HANDS ON
SPINNING

Lee Raven

Illustrations by Ann Sabin

For Mike and Sam

Photography by Joe Coca
Typesetting by Marc McCoy Owens and Chris Hausman
Cover by Signorella Graphic Arts

Interweave Press, Inc.
201 East Fourth Street
Loveland, Colorado 80537
USA

Library of Congress Catalog Number 86-83427
ISBN #0-934026-27-0

Library of Congress Cataloging-in-Publication Data

Raven, Lee, 1950–
    Hands on spinning.

    Bibliography: p.
    Includes index.
    1. Hand spinning.   I. Title.

TT847.R38 1987   746.1'2   86-83427
ISBN 0-934026-27-0 (pbk.)

First Printing: 10M:887:AWO/AC
Second Printing: 10M:189:CP
Third Printing: 10M:991:CP
Fourth Printing: 5M:195:CP

CONTENTS

Projects

Introduction

This book could easily have been subtitled "How to Spin a Good Yarn", for surely its aim is to teach you just that—to make a simple and useful product of skillful manufacture and enduring performance.

For centuries upon centuries, spinning a good yarn was taken for granted. It was something every girlchild and woman did without ceasing from the time she could hold a spindle. It was as common as sweeping the floor, or making soap, or harvesting grain. After the coming of the Industrial Revolution, it took less than ten generations for us to set aside and forget skills that had been refined for over ten millennia.

No one knows when spinning began—10,000 B.C.? 15,000 B.C.? The oldest fabric we know of so far shows that its maker already had remarkable skill. It was found in Turkey and is believed to have been made around 6300 B.C. Far newer fabrics, almost 4500 years old, were made with such precision and skill that they have yet to be duplicated by hand or machine. These are the Egyptian "transparent" linens (there is some dispute over the actual fiber used) with more than five hundred threads to the inch. These and countless other striking textiles all began with yarns spun on a handspindle. Spinning wheels wouldn't be seen for another 3500 years.

It is interesting to note that we have left behind untold numbers of spinning fibers, because of their restricted growing habitat or limited uses, or because they couldn't be economically produced and spun by industry. On the other hand, we spinners have available to us today a mind-boggling array of spinnable fibers to choose from, including the silks, wools, cottons, and flax that you have probably heard of, and fibers like ramie, henequen, musk ox, and camel down that are a little more obscure. We have access to unusual and luxurious fibers from every corner of the world; it could be said, then, that we have much more to learn than did our diligent ancestors.

There is, indeed, very much to learn, both from the ancients and from modern technology, but that is what makes this craft endlessly fascinating and challenging. This little book can't hope to cover the whole craft of spinning, but it will give you the skills and confidence necessary to spin a good yarn. It will teach you the basics of fiber identification, selection, preparation, spinning, finishing, and use. Though it concentrates on wool, you'll be introduced to many other fibers, and the knowledge and skills you gain will be transferable to still others. You will find yourself able to experiment with fiber preparations and with yarn constructions and designs, limited only by your imagination and curiosity.

There is one more thing that I want to impart to you: the sense of fun and satisfaction that can be yours when you begin to master the art of spinning. Like any learned skill, it takes a bit of patience and practice, but the rewards are both immediate and long lasting. There is a fine sense of accomplishment in being able to start with raw fiber and end up with a superior fabric. There is an endless source of experimentation and discovery in seeing the results of dye baths, color and fiber blends, yarn designs, and fabric constructions. Spinning connects you with history, relaxes the tensions of the day with easy rhythms, and gives free rein to your creativity—not a bad bargain at all.

Getting Started

Which fiber is the easiest to learn to spin? Instructors vary considerably in their opinions on which fiber to hand their beginning students. Some will swear by "greasy wool", the fiber just as it is shorn from the sheep, because the fibers are easy to separate, and yet they don't separate too quickly. Others much prefer clean wool, because the fibers slip past one another more uniformly and better spinning control is possible. In Scandinavia, it is common to start new spinners off with "line flax", the long fibers from the stem of the flax plant from which linen is spun. They say that the longer fibers are easier for fumbling fingers to handle. In other countries, novices may learn to spin the fibers that are most readily available, like cotton, hemp, abaca or silk.

My preference is to start students with wool. It is familiar, readily available, inexpensive, easy to handle, and suitable for a wide range of yarn textures and sizes. Students can learn to spin quickly on inexpensive (even homemade) tools, and then knit or crochet a simple woolen hat or scarf with their very first yarn. Clean wool is my first choice, because it is easy to handle, pleasant to use, and gives a better idea of what the final yarn will feel and look like.

There are hundreds of breeds of sheep. You might already be familiar with the fact that different breeds of sheep produce different kinds of wool. Have you seen the word *Merino* on some garments or in fashion magazine advertisements? Merino is a modern breed of sheep, carefully selected and bred over the centuries to produce the softest, finest fibers, suitable for fine fabrics. But even all Merinos are not the same—some have finer or shorter wool than others, and some have brown or black wool instead of white. There are medium-wooled breeds, long-wooled breeds, coarse-wooled breeds, and breeds that are grown for their meat and not their wool at all.

The wool fabrics that you feel in the stores have been through quite a bit of industrial processing, and may contain a number of additives for things like easier laundering, permanent creasing, or mothproofing; but even there you can begin to train yourself to feel which wools are better suited to rugs, and which are going to feel comfortable near your skin. Freshly washed unprocessed wool will give you a more accurate feeling for its softness and comfort or durability. Your fingers can be trained to discern the "hand" of the fiber or fabric, and in that way you can begin to get an idea of the kinds of wool you would like to work with.

Wool In Your Hands

You may already have some wool on hand—perhaps you are growing a few sheep yourself, or you know of someone who is. If you are lucky enough to have a fleece already, great. You can start off with that. You can choose to try spinning "in the grease" if you want to, meaning that you'll spin the wool without washing it. I think you'll find spinning washed or "scoured" wool easier, though, and more pleasant, so let me direct you to the washing instructions in the appendix. Before you wash the wool, you might want to sort it—you'll find instructions in the appendix for that as well. Wash up some wool as directed, and you'll be ready to begin.

If you don't have a source of washed or greasy wool, there are several places you might try. Look in the Yellow Pages under "Weaving —Looms" for spinning and weaving shops. If they don't have fleeces right there, they can often direct you to local wool growers who sell to handspinners. Or call your county extension agent listed in the phone book under "County Government" for the names of small flock owners in your area. Weaving shops also may have on hand a wool preparation called "card sliver", a thick rope-like strand of mill-cleaned and carded wool, ready to spin. You might even run into "carded batts", thick cushiony squares of clean and carded wool, also ready to spin. Either one of those preparations is fine to start with, too.

Ask your local spinning and weaving supplier about local spinning

Teasing wool makes it open and fluffy, so it's easier to spin. The left hand here holds a small clump of unteased fibers. The right hand lightly plucks at the fibers to loosen them, and then the completed fibers are tucked out of the way in the right palm.

When you are ready to spin, pinch a small group of fibers and begin to pull them out from the fiber mass.

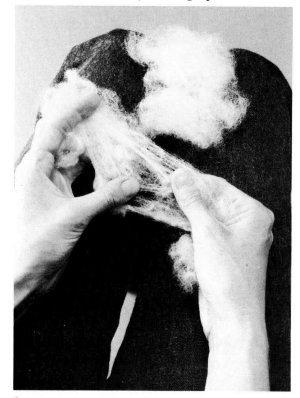

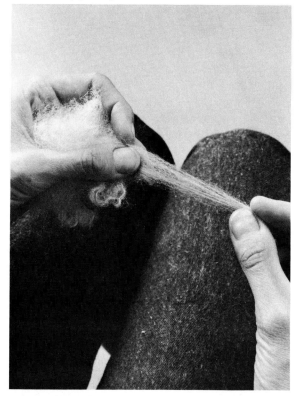

guilds. The guild members will not only be able to help you with finding a fleece (or part of one), they will undoubtedly be delighted to have you join the guild and will offer spinning help.

Spinning and weaving shops usually carry several publications related to spinning, in which you will find many ads for fleeces. Look especially for *Spin·Off* (a colorful quarterly magazine for handspinners), and then for *Black Sheep Newsletter* (a newsprint periodical for spinners and for sheep raisers who specialize in black, brown and gray wools), and *Handwoven* (a full color periodical for handweavers that contains articles of interest to spinners as well). the addresses of these and other publications are listed in the back of the book under "Sources". Look in the classifieds ads of the magazines for wool growers specializing in fleeces for handspinning. Send for samples via the mail, or call or visit the shepherd. "Fleece Selection and Evaluation" in the appendix will help you know what to look for.

You can get a "spinning kit", containing one or more types of wool and a handspindle for you to try, from several sources. these will be adequate for getting started. Again, look in the advertisements in the magazines listed above.

Beginning to Spin

Now that you've got a bit of wool, the only other tools you'll need to get started are your two hands. Begin with a small handful of the wool you have. Gently and gradually separate the fibers from one another so that they are uniformly open and relatively untangled. Your object is simply to separate the fibers from one another so that each one will freely slip past its neighbors when you need it to. When your fibers are teased open, you are ready to spin.

Now. Hold the mass of fibers gently and loosely in one hand. With the other hand, pinch a small group of fibers (say ten to twenty or so, just to give you and idea) and begin to pull them out from the fiber mass, about an inch and a half. Don't pull so hard or so long that you separate these fibers from the rest of the fiber mass—you want to be able to manipulate their front ends just now, but you want their hind ends to stay buried in the mass of wool, or **fiber supply**. What you have just done is called **drafting** fibers, in preparation for **twisting** them into yarn.

Lay the extended fiber ends against your thigh. Hold them all together beneath your forefinger. Now twist the fibers by rolling them against your leg as you rub your finger toward your knee. You'll see the drafted fibers twist together and the twist will begin to run up your newly made "yarn" toward the fiber supply. When the twist just reaches the fiber supply, pick the yarn end up—be careful not to let the twist unwind—and bring it back toward your hip for the next roll down your leg.

Before you roll it again, though, gently pull out an additional inch or two of fibers: just give an easy tug on the beginning end of the yarn. Be sure to hold the fiber supply with a light touch so that the fibers can slip as you need them to; you don't want to be playing tug-of-war on either end of the same fibers. If you watch closely, you'll see some of the twist that you've put in your "yarn" begin to run into the newly drafted fibers. Now, just as before, hold the beginning end of the yarn under your forefinger and roll it down your leg.

You have just made yarn! You have performed the two basic actions required of spinning: **drafting** and **twisting** fibers. There are many more things to learn about making these actions more rapid and efficient, but you have successfully completed the two most vital steps for making yarn. The process is almost deceptive in its simplicity, yet you'll find that no matter how far you go in this craft, the magic is never really lost.

Continue as you were before, keeping the yarn taut as you draft and then roll. In that way, the twist can move, or "travel", along the length of the yarn, evening itself out instead of building up in one place. Be sure you always twist in the same direction, and that you keep the twisted end from undoing itself.

As you continue you'll see the yarn growing and your two hands moving farther and farther apart, the beginning end of the yarn in one hand, the fiber supply in the other. Here's a simple test that will tell you if your yarn is good and strong: keep your hold on the beginning end,

As you roll your finger across the fibers, they will twist together. The twist will run up the extended fibers toward the fiber supply.

After you make a length of yarn, test its strength by holding both ends and pulling gently.

and with your other hand, pinch the yarn just in front of the fiber supply. Now steadily, but gently, try to pull the two ends farther apart. If you feel your hands moving apart, even a little bit, the fibers are slipping past one another; that means the yarn isn't twisted quite enough to bind the fibers together. Here is your **first axiom of spinning:** *If you don't twist the drafted fibers enough, your yarn will drift apart and break.* The remedy? Twist the fibers some more without doing any more drafting, and then test the yarn again. When you can tug gently on both ends of the yarn and nothing happens, then be assured that you have sufficient twist in your yarn to make it sound and strong.

If you are particularly efficient at rolling the yarn end down your leg, you may find that your little length of yarn is twisted so much that drafting more fibers becomes difficult. Which brings us to the **second axiom of spinning:** *If you twist the drafted fibers too much, the twist will travel into the fiber supply, engulfing the whole mass and preventing further drafting.* You can fix this by gradually untwisting the yarn (not the fiber supply) until you can draft again.

So, yes, there are such things as too little and too much twist, but there is a lot of leeway in between, and there will always be tests you can do to judge the right amount of twist for your yarn. For now, if you can keep drafting and twisting bit by bit, and your yarn is holding together, you're doing great.

Well now. What are you going to do with that length of yarn stretched between your hands? How can you secure or store what you have made so that it will not untwist, and so that you can keep adding to its length? One of the first solutions that the ancients came up with was the "hooked stick", a tool still in use today.

Spinning on the Hooked Stick

You can make your own hooked stick by cutting yourself a twelve-inch length of wire coat hanger. Sand the cut ends smooth so that there are no sharp burrs to catch on your hands or on the wool. With some needlenose pliers, bend one end into a shepherd's crook. Bend the hook back a bit so that the topmost curve of the bend is in direct line with the shaft, as shown. This will keep vibrations out of your yarn as you are twisting the stick.

Here's how to start on the hooked stick if you don't already have a length of finger-spun yarn. Take a small handful of wool fiber and tease it gently apart into a uniform mass, as before. With your stick, hook a small group of fibers near the edge of the fiber supply. Holding the shaft of the stick, gently pull out those hooked fibers an inch or two from the fiber supply. Now put the shaft of the stick down on your leg and roll it slowly toward your knee with your fingers and palm. This is a much more efficient way to twist fibers, isn't it? Very rapidly the twist will enter the yarn, and move up to the fiber supply—and that's as far as you want it to go.

Just as before, pick up the stick and move it back toward your hip in preparation for the next roll. Draft an additional length of fibers, about two inches, then roll the shaft down your leg. Always keep the yarn taut so that the twist will distribute itself evenly along the length of

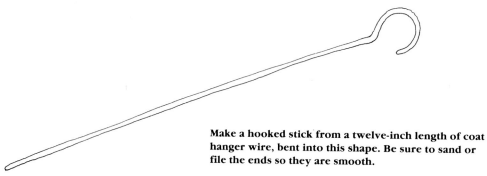

Make a hooked stick from a twelve-inch length of coat hanger wire, bent into this shape. Be sure to sand or file the ends so they are smooth.

the yarn, and so the yarn won't collapse and snarl on itself. Keep a constant hold on both the fiber supply and the stick, or your yarn may untwist. Continue drafting and twisting until you have a couple of feet of yarn.

Winding On

Once you have spun a length of yarn, you will be ready to store that portion on the stick so that you can continue to add to its length. Before you store it, be sure to test the yarn for sufficient twist by giving it a gentle tug between your hands. If it doesn't drift apart, it's ready to be wound on.

Keeping the yarn taut, slip the loop of fibers down from the top of the hook to the middle of the shaft. Hold the loop firmly in place on the middle of the shaft as you begin turning the stick in your hand to wind the yarn around the shaft. Hold the fiber supply stationary, and the yarn taut, while you turn the stick in the *same direction* that you used to twist your yarn. The yarn should be wound firmly (so it doesn't slip loosely around the shaft) in small overlapping turns (to keep it compact) in the center of the shaft. Stop when you have about an eight-inch length of yarn left. Now keep turning the stick in the same direction, but begin to spiral the yarn up the shaft toward the hook in a barber pole pattern. The last wrap should be made directly under the

To begin spinning with the hooked stick, pick up a small group of fibers at the edge of the fiber supply and gently pull this group away from the mass.

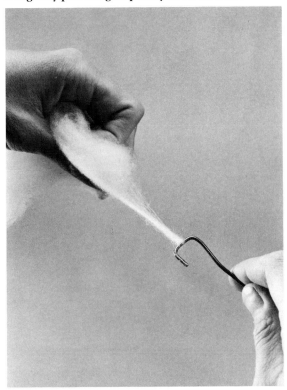

Once again, make sure you have enough twist in your yarn. This piece wasn't twisted enough—it's drifting apart and is about to break.

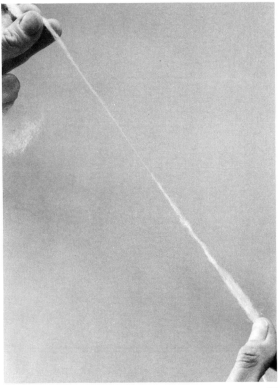

hook. You should have a few inches of yarn extending out from the hook which will form the anchor for your next length of yarn. You are ready to begin again. Go at your own pace, spinning and winding on a few more lengths of yarn.

The Drafting Zone

When you've spun a bit more, hold a length of yarn and the fiber supply out in front of you. Take special note of that small triangular area *between* the yarn and the fiber supply. It's called the **drafting triangle** or the **drafting zone.** It is a transition area where the drafted fibers meet the twist. *That is where yarn is made.* In any kind of spinning, it deserves your constant attention. The size, consistency, texture and character of your yarn are determined in that little space. Watch how the size and shape of the drafting zone change as you work. Drafting new fibers elongates the triangle, and adding twist shortens it; drafting a greater number of fibers thickens the triangle (your yarn becomes thicker as well), and drafting fewer fibers thins it.

Problems

Are you running into any problems? Perhaps the drafting seems difficult. You may be adding too much twist for the number and length of fibers you've drafted. Try this: as you slowly roll the stick down your leg, watch the twist as it travels up the fibers you have drafted. Stop adding twist as it reaches the end of the drafted fibers, just before it

The drafting triangle is where yarn is made. Keep your eye on it—you'll learn a lot!

Wind your yarn firmly onto the center of the hooked stick in the same direction you used to spin your yarn.

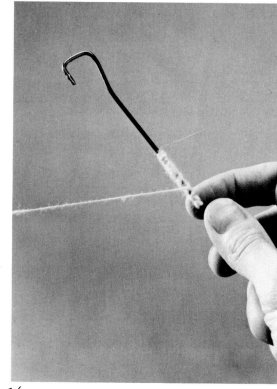

Make your last wrap directly under the hook and you're ready to spin again.

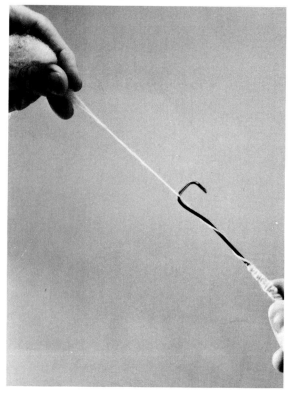

14

starts to enter the fiber supply itself. Once the twist enters the fiber supply, it will try to engulf the whole mass into a gigantic super-yarn. Friction will hold all the twisted fibers together, making drafting just a portion of them difficult or impossible.

If too much twist doesn't seem to be the problem, it may be that your fiber supply is insufficiently teased. Remember that the fibers must be completely free to slip past one another. Loose, open fibers will draft easily.

Another common problem is grasping the fibers too tightly for them to slip past your fingers and into the yarn. First, relax your fingers, and all the muscles clear up into your shoulder. Spinning is a relaxing sport, and you'll have a much easier time of it if you remind yourself to keep everything loose. You may also be holding the fibers too close to the drafting zone. With the twist firmly holding one end of the fibers, and your fingers firmly holding the other end of the very same fibers, what you have is a tug-of-war, not drafting. Hold the fiber supply delicately, and several inches back from the drafting zone.

Does the yarn itself just slip apart when you try to draft, instead of pulling along new fibers out of the supply? Then you need more twist to hold your yarn together. Make sure the twist travels all the way up to the edge of the main fiber supply before you draft additional fibers. The compressing friction of the twist has to move up and grasp a few more fiber ends so that they will be pulled along into the next drafted section. Be sure you're holding the fiber supply loosely so that you're

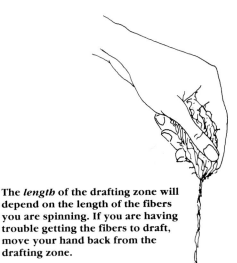

If the twist enters the fiber supply, you will find it difficult or impossible to draft. Keep the twist out of the drafting zone.

The *length* of the drafting zone will depend on the length of the fibers you are spinning. If you are having trouble getting the fibers to draft, move your hand back from the drafting zone.

Lumps are common. Sometimes you'll want them, and sometimes you won't. Right now, don't worry about them. Twist accumulates in thin places and skips over thick ones.

not inadvertently preventing the fibers from moving into the yarn.

What about all those lumps in the yarn? For heaven's sake, don't worry about smoothness yet—that will come with practice. Lumps happen for a variety of reasons, but basically they form because the same number of fibers did not continuously pass through the drafting zone at a constant speed, commensurate with the advancing twist. That just means that the fat places are where too many fibers came through as a bunch, and the thin places are where too few came through. Sometimes a lump is a group of short fibers traveling as a clump, or a tangle of fibers around a sticker or burr. It might be a clump of longer fibers incompletely teased, or maybe a place where the twist got away from you and just grabbed too many fibers at once. All those conditions will be completely under your control with practice in fiber preparation and spinning technique. And remember, sometimes it's all in the way you look at it. Some spinners interested in novelty effects encourage the thick-and-thin look as a design element.

We talked about keeping the yarn taut so that twist would not accumulate in one place, but would travel the length of the yarn and even itself out. It's important for you to note, however, what happens to the twist when the yarn is unevenly spun. Take a look at the fatter places in your yarn. The twist stubbornly refuses to travel through the thicker portions, even when the yarn is held taut. Instead, it accumulates in the thinner sections. This is a property of yarn structure, and you'll find it to be true no matter what fiber you are spinning. Given that property, there is something to be said for keeping your yarns reasonably even. When they are, their strength and abrasion resistance is not only more uniform throughout the length of the yarn, it is actually higher overall. But for now, your aim is just to make a sound yarn: one that doesn't drift apart, and one that doesn't snarl upon itself uncontrollably.

Do you have a particularly large lump that you would really like to get rid of? Here's a trick of the trade for you. Put down the hooked stick and the fiber supply. Take hold of the yarn on either side of the offending lump, about an inch or so away from where it thickens. Turn your hands so that the yarn between them begins to untwist, just to the point where you can feel it begin to drift apart. Gently stretch the lump (the fibers in the lump will begin to slide past one another) until you reduce it to the size you want. Let the yarn go and watch the twist run into the newly stretched portion. (If you can't get the lump to start drifting, your hands are too close together. Move them slightly farther apart and try again.)

Drafting and Twisting Simultaneously

When you begin to feel comfortable with drafting and twisting in sequence, try combining the two steps. As you slowly add twist by rolling the stick down your leg, draft the fibers at the same time by pulling gently back on the fiber supply, letting some fibers slip through. Be sure to keep your eyes on the twist and how it travels; you'll need to add twist at the same rate that you draft fibers, letting neither process get ahead of the other. The twist should consistently enter the drafted fibers just an inch or so in front of the fiber supply. Try spinning a short length of yarn in this manner and then test it for soundness.

As you continue to draft and twist simultaneously, keep your eyes on the drafting zone. Ideally, a spinner wants to keep the same number of fibers entering the zone at one end while the twist enters the fibers at the same point on the other end. If the drafting triangle elongates, then the twisting rate is falling behind the drafting rate. If the triangle foreshortens, then the twist rate is outpacing the drafting rate. See how close you can come to keeping the drafting triangle constant in size and shape, and take note of what happens to your yarn as that zone varies.

There is a relationship between the size of the yarn you want to make and the amount of twist required to hold it together. Here's the **third axiom of spinning** for you: *The fewer the number of fibers that you draft, and thus the finer the diameter of the yarn, the more twist you will need to hold it together.* Conversely, the more fibers and the thicker the yarn, the less twist will be required to bind the fibers together. Test this for yourself, spinning thinner and thicker yarns, checking them for soundness, and observing their changing character as more or less twist is used.

Fewer fibers? You'll need more twist.

Lots of fibers? A smaller amount of twist will hold the yarn together.

Direction of Twist—Z and S

Yarn can be twisted in one of two directions, either clockwise or counterclockwise, right or left. Think of the beginning of your yarn, the point where you first begin to twist it, as rotating in one or the other direction. If you sight down the line of your yarn, from the fiber supply to the hook, you'll see that the hook (which holds the beginning of your yarn on its shaft) can turn to the right (clockwise) giving you what is called a "Z-twist" yarn, or it can turn to the left (counterclockwise) giving you what is called an "S-twist" yarn. No matter what tool twists the yarn—your hand, a stick, a spindle or a spinning wheel—the direction that the beginning rotates (even if it is hidden under layers of newly spun yarn) determines twist direction.

If you take a look at the drawings here you'll see that the Z-twist yarn is so named because the fibers slant in the same direction as the downward stroke of the letter Z. Can you see in your mind's eye that twisting the top of this imaginary yarn to the right, while holding the bottom stationary, would give you that result? What would happen if it were twisted to the left? An S-twist yarn, with the fibers slanting in the same direction as the downward stroke of the letter S.

Take a look at your own yarn. S or Z? Which way did the beginning rotate? If you held the fiber supply in your left hand and rolled the stick down your right leg (toward your knee), then your yarn would be S twisted, because the hook rolled counterclockwise. If the fibers were held in your right hand and you rolled the stick down your left leg, your yarn would be Z twisted. What would your own yarn be if you rolled the stick *up* your leg, toward your hip?

Now here's an interesting experiment and an important point to remember. Turn this book upside down and take another look at the Z-

Z   **S**

Z

S

S is S, and Z is Z, whether right side up or upside down.

and S-twist yarn sketches (and for that matter, at the letters themselves). No matter which way you look at them, upside down or rightside up, a Z yarn is always a Z yarn, and an S yarn always an S yarn. Prove it to yourself with your own handspun; turn it every which way you can. Whether you started out with a Z- or an S-twist yarn, that is what it will remain.

That's good to know for a couple of reasons. First, when you get into **plying** (twisting two or more yarns together), you'll need to know in which direction your original yarns were spun, but it won't matter if you mix up the starting or finishing end. Once a Z, always a Z. And later on, once you start using your handspun in knitting, crocheting and weaving, you'll find that Z- and S-twist yarns act a bit differently in certain situations, but no matter what convolutions you put them through in making your fabric, their twist directions will always remain the same.

Most of today's spinners tend to spin most of their singles yarns (as opposed to plied yarns) in the Z direction. This seems to be true all over the world—where spinning is still a regular part of a woman's workday, where it is pursued as an art and craft, or where it is industrialized (though you'll always find exceptions). Realize, however, that essentially there is no difference in a Z- or an S-spun yarn—they both do the job equally well—and you are free to spin in whatever direction pleases you. It's a good idea to be consistent in the direction you choose, though, so that you don't have to spend a lot of time examining your yarns when you pick them up later for use in a plied yarn or a new fabric.

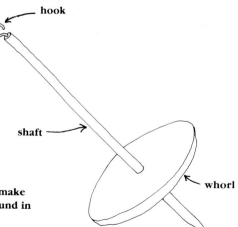

The hand spindle, which you can make yourself, is an ancient tool still found in use.

Speeding It Up: Using the Hand Spindle

Hand spindles have been used for uncounted generations, and can be found in use throughout the world to this day. In some countries they are used exclusively because of their minimum size and maximum portability; yarn can be spun throughout the day amidst other activities, resulting in good yarn production with no interruption of other necessary tasks.

The hand spindle is a simple extension of the idea of the hooked stick. You just add a small weight to increase momentum, stand it upright and give it a good spin, and your speed and production can be markedly increased. Most spindles consist of a wooden shaft with a small weight attached near one end. Shafts can be anywhere from eight to thirty-six inches long, but the most common measure is in the neighborhood of twelve to fifteen inches long. Many are tapered to a dull point near the weight at one end, with a carved or an attached hook at the other end; others are gradually tapered at both ends. The weight, called a **whorl,** is a disk or ball of wood, stone or clay with a hole in the middle. The whorl is slipped onto the end of the spindle shaft, opposite the hook, and is usually held in place by friction.

You can buy a variety of modern spindles at spinning and weaving shops, or through the mail (see the appendices), or you can make your own. There are a few things to keep in mind, either way. The shaft should be straight and smooth; you want it to rotate without vibration, and to be free of rough places that will catch on your yarn. Although some spindles end in just a smooth taper at each end, your efficiency can be increased if there is a hook. Most often, the hook will be at the opposite end of the shaft from the whorl. Spindles with the hook at the same end of the shaft as the whorl are called high top or high whorl spindles, and even greater spinning speeds can be achieved with them. The whorl should be round and evenly balanced, so that when the spindle is turning, it won't wobble and thereby lose speed too quickly.

Making Your Own Hand Spindle

Here are some possibilities for making your own spindles. Shafts can be made from one-quarter inch or three-eighth inch dowels found at the hardware store. You can cut the dowels to length, or sometimes find them ready to go in twelve-inch sections. Sand one end to a steep, rounded cone shape. The spindle should be able to rest on that end and

Colonial hand spindle

Spindle with painted whorl

Turkish spindle

spin freely, much like a top. Sand the other end just to get rid of the rough edges.

To make a hook, screw a cup hook exactly in the center of the end of the shaft. A small pilot hole made with a punch will help keep the shaft from splitting when you screw in the hook. You can also hand carve a simple hook shape into the end of your spindle, as shown. Take note, however, that this will introduce a slight wobble into your rotating spindle. That is because the yarn will be coming off the side of the spindle shaft instead of directly from its center axis. A better method is to make two cuts with a hack saw, one straight down into the end of the shaft about a half inch long, and a second cut, made 90° away into the side of the shaft, angling up to meet the first cut (see illustration). Thus you have a modified "T" cut in that end of the shaft. The yarn will slide into one short arm of the T and then up the line of the first cut to emerge out of the center of the shaft. Be sure and sand away any rough edges.

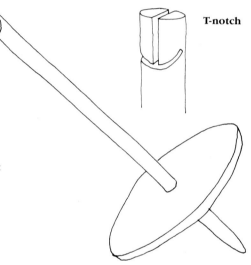

T-notch

One way to get a hook at the top of your spindle shaft is to use a cup hook.

A modified T-notch allows the yarn to come straight up from the center of the shaft. This less-common design prevents some of the slight wobble which occurs as a spindle rotates.

Your whorl can be made from a solid wood coaster (like those found at import stores), or from a two or three inch wooden wheel found at a hobby store, or from a large wooden drawer pull. If there's a woodworker handy, a two or three inch disk can be cut with a bandsaw from one-half or five-eighths inch thick solid wood or plywood, and then trued to round on a lathe. You may even be able to get away with sanding it round, but be very accurate. If you need to drill a hole in the center of your whorl, be sure to do it in the exact center, so that it will be properly balanced when it rotates.

The whorl needs to fit *tightly* on the shaft, about an inch and a half or so up from the rounded end (opposite the hook). If you choose to glue it in position, that's fine, as long as the fit is fairly firm to begin with. Another solution is to make the hole in the whorl slightly smaller than the shaft diameter, and then sand that end of the shaft down gradually until the whorl fits where you want it to by friction. Taper it so that it is smallest at the tip, larger as you go toward the body. If you've got a whorl with a hole in it already that seems just a wee bit large for the job, you can wrap a bit of unspun wool around the shaft and then fit the whorl on over that. Be sure it's tight.

You can see that there are a lot of possibilities here for variation; you've probably already thought of some on your own. Spindle shafts have been made from scrap lumber, carved tree branches, brass or iron rods, and bamboo. Spindle whorls have been made from pottery shards, soft clay, metal disks, and even rocks. Your shafts and whorls can be as fancy or as simple as you choose. As far as size variations go, in very general terms, the smaller the spindle, the finer the yarn, and the larger the spindle, the greater the size of the yarn.

Test your spindle for smooth rotation by placing the end with the whorl on the table, and giving the top of the shaft a hearty spin. Keep it upright by loosely enclosing the top of the shaft with a circle of your fingers and thumb allowing it to freely spin. You'll need a bit of practice to get the hang of turning the spindle efficiently. If it turns smoothly like a top, you're in business. A little wobble is fine—don't worry. But if your spindle has a lot of wobble in it and slows down quickly, you'd best try again.

Hand Spindle Spinning

For consistency's sake, and for the clarity of the instructions to follow, spin your yarns with a Z twist, turning the spindle in a clockwise direction. I suggest that you use your right hand to manipulate the spindle, and your left to hold the fibers.

Make a starter yarn or **leader,** about two and a half feet long, out of your own finger-spun yarn, just as we did in the beginning. (Hold the fiber supply in your left hand, and roll the yarn *up* your leg from knee to hip for a Z-twist yarn.) Leave it attached to the fiber supply. Holding the yarn taut, take the beginning of your yarn and wrap it firmly around the shaft of your spindle immediately above the whorl. Hold the yarn stationary and rotate the spindle clockwise to wrap the yarn. Wrap it around four or five times to secure it, and then begin spiraling it up the shaft in a barber pole pattern, just as you did with the hooked stick. Wrap the yarns fairly close, an inch or less apart, for a better grip on the shaft. Leave several inches of yarn to extend beyond the end of the hook. If you have used the cup hook or the simple carved hook, just take the last wrap directly underneath the hook. If you have made the T hook, slide the yarn into one short arm of the T and then up and out the center of the shaft.

In the case of a hand spindle that has no hook at the top, a half-hitch knot is sometimes recommended. The yarn is brought from its wind-on point down *under* the whorl, wrapped once around the shaft, and brought back up over the whorl to the top of the shaft, where a half hitch secures it to the shaft before spinning commences. Two of the problems that can occur with this method are that 1) the spindle

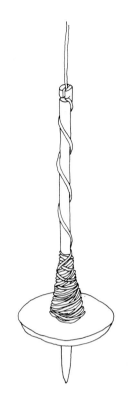

If your spindle has no hook, secure the end of your leader with a half-hitch.

may not rotate smoothly because the yarn is coming from the side instead of the center of the shaft, and that 2) turning the spindle efficiently with your hand is made more difficult because the yarn is not closely wrapped to the shaft, but stands out from it.

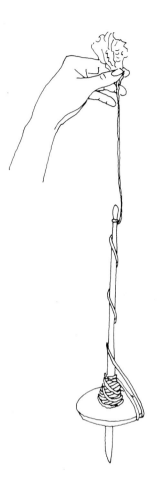

To make a half-hitch, you can loop the leader around your finger and then slide the tip of your spindle through the loop.

Supported Spindle

Let's begin by using this as a **supported spindle.** Rest the lower tip of the spindle on a table top or other convenient smooth surface while you hold up the top of the spindle with your right hand. This gives the double advantage of supporting the weight of the spindle (so its heaviness doesn't try to pull your yarn apart), and discouraging the spindle from unwinding (and thus unspinning your yarn) after it's slowed to a stop. Hold the yarn taut with the left hand, and use the right hand to give the top of the spindle shaft a gentle twist in a clockwise direction. Use a circle of thumb and finger to keep the top of the spindle upright while allowing it to turn freely. As the spindle is turning and adding more twist, draft more fibers for the twist to move into. You'll have to draft a bit faster now, because the twist is being added faster. When you're using a supported spindle, you'll find that drafting is easier if you draft new fibers just *before* the twist has reached the fiber supply—keep the fibers flowing very loosely. You can always add extra twist later to ensure a sound yarn.

When the spindle slows almost to a stop, keep the yarn taut, and reach down and give the shaft another clockwise twist. Don't let it stop and begin to unwind.

As you work, watch the drafting zone, trying for a smooth flow of fibers meeting the advancing twist. Don't expect to be spinning perfect yarn here—none of us did at this stage! Just work for better and better control with your fingers as you practice.

If drafting seems difficult or very uneven, there is a way you can use both hands to help. Once the spindle is turning, you can reach up with the spindle hand and tug very quickly on the yarn below the drafting zone to help you past a difficult spot. Don't hang on to the yarn more than a moment, though, because the twist will not be able to travel past your pinching fingers. The yarn's tautness will help the spindle stay upright. Just as before, when the spindle slows significantly, reach down and give it another twirl.

Winding On

To wind your yarn on, hold it taut while you turn the spindle shaft counterclockwise, unwinding the yarn spiraled around the shaft. (Did you remember to test it for soundness?) When you get to the end of the spirals, reverse direction again and begin winding on what you have just spun. Wind it all near the bottom of the shaft at the whorl. When you have about fifteen inches or so of yarn left, begin to spiral the yarn up the shaft and under the hook, leaving a few inches extending beyond the spindle tip to start your next length. Draft a bit of fiber, spin the spindle, and off you go again.

As you wind on more lengths of your handspun yarn, build up a cone shape of the yarn, called a **cop,** on the spindle as you go. The widest part of the cone should be sitting on the whorl, and it should taper steeply to the shaft. Keep the cone wide and short, to encourage the weight of the yarn to be as near the whorl as possible. This helps to

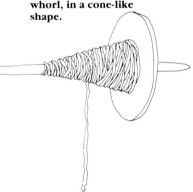

Wind yarn onto the spindle at its base, near the whorl, in a cone-like shape.

To use your drop spindle as a supported spindle, make a ring of your thumb and forefinger and keep the spindle shaft upright as it spins.

While the spindle is turning, you can reach up quickly with the spindle hand and help yourself over a tough spot. Be sure to keep some tension on the yarn so the spindle won't fall over.

increase your spinning momentum, and leaves the shaft free for your fingers to turn it. Taking care in the winding on process to make a smooth tapering cone will make it easier for you to retrieve your yarn from the spindle when it is full.

As you practice, you ought to be able to give the spindle more and more energetic twists so that it doesn't slow down quite so quickly. The faster you turn the spindle, the faster your drafting fingers will have to be.

Drop Spindle

Very quickly, though, you'll be ready to try your spindle as a **drop spindle.** Instead of supporting it on a table, let it hang and twist freely in the air, dropping gradually to the ground as your yarn lengthens. Proceed just as you did before, giving the spindle a good clockwise twist. This time, though, let the spindle drop away from you, and use both hands nearer the drafting zone: the left to control the fiber supply, and the right, about a foot below it, to tug downward gently on the newly spun yarn itself. This is good practice since the weight of the spindle and the gentle tug of your right hand is somewhat like the tug you'll feel at the spinning wheel.

Remind yourself to let the twist travel through your fingers after each quick tug or your yarn will slip apart from lack of twist. Your yarn now has to be strong enough to support the weight of the spindle, so it will constantly need the strength that twist imparts. Resist the temptation to reach into the drafting zone itself to help a reluctant flow of fibers; you are likely to cause the yarn to separate suddenly or to become increasingly lumpy. It's a bad habit you don't want to acquire.

Keep on spinning lengths and winding them on until you have nearly a full spindle of handspun.

Broken Yarns

If your yarn is breaking and the spindle suddenly dropping to the ground, it's because there is not enough twist in the yarn to hold it together. You may have let the yarn get too thin (thinner yarn needs more twist to hold together), or you may have kept the twist from getting past your fingers into the drafted portion of fibers. Sometimes spinners will concentrate so intensely on the forming yarn that they forget to check the progress of the turning spindle down below. If it stops and then begins to unwind, your yarn will untwist and fall apart.

Don't worry, though. There will be many times to come when you'll want to mend a broken end or add new fiber to an existing end of yarn. All you have to do is make a **join.**

Making Joins

A join should be a smooth, invisible melding of fibers that is just as strong as the rest of your yarn. You do this by overlapping a fluff of fibers from the end of the yarn to a fluff of fibers attached to the fiber supply, drafting the two fluffs together to the size of yarn you want,

When you stand up to use the spindle, you'll be able to spin a greater length of yarn before you need to wind on.

and then letting them twist together. Place the new fibers over the old fibers by two or three inches, pinch each edge of the join, draft to the appropriate size, and let the twist from the yarn run into the join. Add more twist by spinning the spindle, and then continue spinning the new length of yarn.

It is very important that you don't try to make a join by twisting a new fluff of fibers over an already spun portion of yarn, for then the new fibers are merely laid on the top of the old yarn, and will easily slip or abrade off. Instead, join unspun fibers to unspun fibers, *draft them together,* and then add twist.

To get a nice fluffy section at the end of your yarn, just untwist the fibers and spread them out. Sometimes this is easiest if you go back several inches to a place where there is a natural thickening of the yarn, a **slub.** Untwist your yarn there and fluff out the fiber ends for the join (just break off and discard the few intervening inches of yarn).

Test your join by pulling gently on the yarn to either side to be sure the join doesn't slip apart. Then run your fingers back and forth over the join; if you see a group of fibers being pushed up into a little bundle, your join is not quite secure. Start over, joining fluff to fluff.

Joins are so important, and will be needed so often, that you should really stop and practice several now. Not only will you have broken ends occasionally, but you'll find yourself wanting to add different fibers or different colors when you begin to explore yarn design. Get your joins down right in the beginning, and you'll be much happier

Make a good join by overlapping two fluffs of fiber and drafting them together.

Let the twist run into the join, then add more twist by spinning the spindle before you continue making the new length of yarn.

with the serviceability of your yarn from now on. A broken yarn from a bad join in the middle of your project is highly frustrating.

More Problems and Solutions

If the yarn seems to be getting too thin, slow down your drafting slightly and let the twist build up a bit, so that more fibers are caught in the twist and pulled along into the forming yarn. If your yarn is getting too thick, draft a little faster, and slow down the twist by turning the spindle a little slower. Make your changes gradually so that you can control them more easily.

If you can't get the fibers to draft, then you may still be grasping them too firmly and too near the drafting zone. Relax your fingers and move them a couple of inches back into the fiber supply. I know that it can feel as if you are asking for disaster if you don't tightly control those fibers just as they enter the drafting zone; it feels as if they will slip through too quickly, separating the yarn and sending the spindle crashing to the floor. But what you must strive for here is the feeling that you got when you were working with the hooked stick: the fibers slipping easily through the drafting triangle just as the twist was entering them. Let the sensitivity in your fingers tell you when the fibers are loose enough to slip, but not so loose that the twist can't immediately catch them.

Don't worry about your yarn being uneven at this point. Slubs, those thicker places in your yarn, are found in every spinner's first

Your join will not be secure if you try to lap a fluff over a section of spun yarn. It may hold and you may be able to successfully continue spinning.

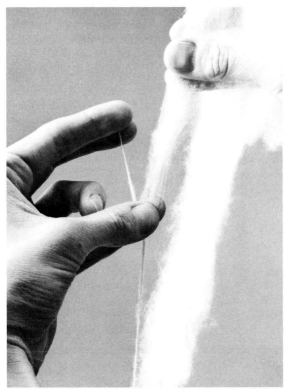

However, when you test the join by pulling the yarn or by rubbing your fingers across the overlapped section, you will discover that the yarn is not sound.

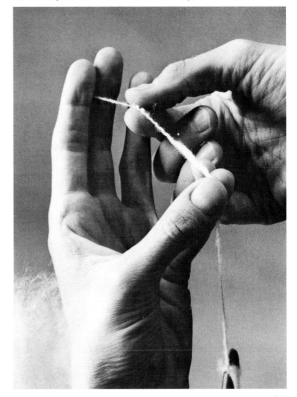

efforts. Just work toward that feeling of smoothly flowing fibers, and that in turn will smooth out the size of your yarn. If a slub is just too big to ignore, stop and untwist it from both ends until the fibers are parallel, draft the fibers to the correct size, and then let the twist re-enter the yarn. Places that are too thin cannot be corrected satisfactorily except by more drastic measures: breaking the yarn, and finding a good place to make a join.

Don't be too frustrated if you just can't seem to get things going right away. You hands are very busy indeed, and you've been given a lot of things to remember and do at once. It's quite natural to feel a bit clumsy at this stage. For now, your head has to tell your fingers and hands every little move to make, but soon you will start spinning more by touch—it just takes practice. The solution is to slow things down a bit until things start feeling more natural. One of the best ways to do this is to recruit a friend. One of you should get down on one knee in front of the other, and take over the duties of spinning the spindle. Go slowly at first, and take directions from the standing spinner. She, meanwhile, can concentrate solely on drafting fibers and controlling twist. When you both feel comfortable in your roles, switch around, and get used to the other position. Then, of course, it is time to try both parts together. If you don't have someone near who can help, go back briefly to the hooked stick and the supported spindle. Be patient with yourself, and relax. You are learning a new patterning, a new skill with your hands; it takes time and a bit of practice, but everyone can do it.

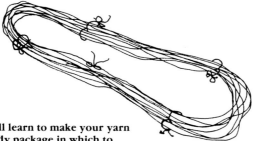

In the next chapter, you will learn to make your yarn into a skein, which is a handy package in which to process or store it.

Processing Your First Yarn

When you have a spindle full of yarn, you'll be ready to wind it off into a **skein,** in order to measure its length and keep it manageable, and then to wash it, to **set the twist.** Winding the yarn into a skein, much like winding a rope or a garden hose into a loose coil, keeps the yarn orderly and easy to handle. You'll also want to set the twist in the yarn permanently, so you don't have to worry about it trying to untwist or tangle on itself later.

First you'll want to be sure that the yarn will pull off smoothly from the spindle. If your cone of yarn is wound neatly, you'll find that the yarn will pull directly off the tip of the spindle; you have only to secure the spindle in an upright position so that your hands are free to wind and direct the yarn. If you have used a cup hook at the top of the spindle, you may find that the yarn gets caught in the hook when it tries to unwind. In that case, wind the yarn off from the side of the spindle shaft, much as you would unwind a spool of thread. Take a cardboard box and make two notches in it to hold the spindle horizontally. It will then rotate easily as you pull the yarn, leaving your hands free.

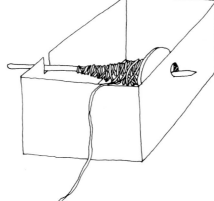

A cardboard box will support your spindle as you wind the yarn off.

Winding the Skein

An easy way to wind your yarn into a skein is to just use the back of a chair. Hold the end of the yarn securely in one place, and wind the yarn from your spindle around and around the back of the chair. Don't wind it too tightly, just use moderate and even tension—you want to be able to lift the whole skein from the back of the chair when you're done. When you come to the end of the yarn, tie it to the beginning (completing the circle) in a firm bow tie.

A chair with straight sides provides a handy form for skein-winding.

Now cut four six-inch lengths of scrap yarn, and tie figure-8 ties at four points on the skein as shown. You'll need these ties only temporarily while you wash the skein to help keep it orderly in the bath; otherwise you can end up with a terrible tangle.

Before you remove the skein from the back of the chair, do two more things. Measure the distance around the chair with a tape measure (in inches), and then count the number of loops in the skein (that is to say, the number of revolutions the yarn made around the chair back). Multiply the first number by the second, and you will have the length of your yarn in inches. Divide by 36, and you'll have a measure of your yardage. It's important to keep track of the number of yards you have available. Soon, you will get a feeling for how many yards it takes for your first simple projects, like hats, scarves and mittens, and by keeping track of your skeins, you'll know how much you have on hand, and how much you have left to spin.

Pictured here is a *niddy noddy* ("niddy" for short), a device of ancient origin used to simultaneously measure yardage and make a skein. Niddy noddies come in various sizes, and can be crude or elegant, but most are made so that the skein length will be some portion of a yard (e.g., ½ yard, 1 yard, 1½ yards, or 2 yards). Thus you have only to count the revolutions you make in going around the niddy and multiply by the niddy's size to have your yardage.

A figure-8 tie keeps the strands of yarn from tangling. Use at least three ties per skein. The "waist" of the figure-8 puts roughly half the strands in each bundle; a precise division isn't necessary or desirable.

Some niddies are fancy, and some are not. The one on the right is as elegant as they come. Whether plain or ornate, every niddy has a center post, which you hold, and two end pieces (set at right angles both to the center post and to each other) around which you wind your yarn.

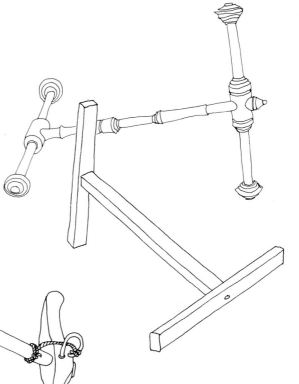

To use the niddy noddy, hold the yarn end against the center shaft with your left hand. Use your right hand to guide the yarn around: first up and over the arm to the right, down and under the arm to the rear, up and over the arm to the left, and finally, down and under the arm in front to complete the circuit. You'll have to twist and turn the niddy a little with your wrist as you go, but don't loosen your grip on the beginning of the yarn and the center shaft. Keep travelling in the same path over and over until you run out of yarn and can tie the beginning and the end together. Double check that you followed the path correctly all the way through by looking for crossed threads. Make your figure-8 ties as before, and slip the skein off the arms of the niddy noddy. (Sometimes the arms are removeable to assist you, sometimes the arm ends are just rounded down so you can slip the skein off easily.)

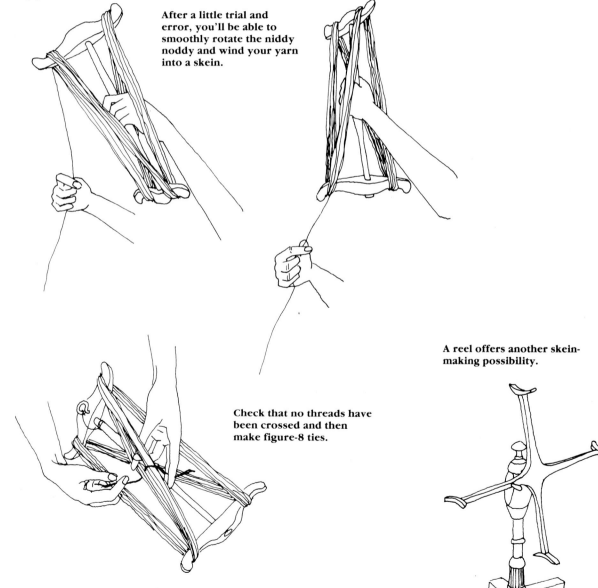

After a little trial and error, you'll be able to smoothly rotate the niddy noddy and wind your yarn into a skein.

Check that no threads have been crossed and then make figure-8 ties.

A reel offers another skein-making possibility.

Spinners also use **reels** to make skeins, like the one pictured here. They are not necessary, however—just a convenience for someone producing a lot of yarn.

Setting the Twist

Setting the twist in yarns is done in a variety of ways depending on the fiber used. For wool yarns, the process is fast and simple. First fill a dishpan half full of very warm water (just comfortable to the hand) and some mild dishwashing detergent (don't make suds). Use only a little detergent if your fiber was clean to begin with, more if you started with greasy wool. Lay your skein on top of the water and let it sink as it absorbs water. Don't worry if your skein looks like a bunch of curly springs—the ties will help you keep it orderly. Just let the skein soak there for a few minutes to be sure the water has fully penetrated the fibers. This will also clean any excess dirt or oils on the wool.

Do not be tempted to wring, scrub or twist the skein, because too much agitation, especially in the presence of heat and moisture, will cause your yarn to felt together—and the felting process is not reversible. For the same reason, you want to avoid running water directly onto your yarn. You may, however, gently squeeze the skein once or twice, or stir it in the water, being careful to avoid excess tangling.

You may notice that the yarn fluffs up or **lofts** a bit in the water—that is to be expected, and is desired by knitters and crocheters because it produces a yarn with a better **hand** (a softer, loftier feel). It is caused by the wool fibers relaxing, trying to get back to their original crimpy shape as they were on the sheep. This is an added benefit to this yarn finishing process.

Now lift the skein out of the wash bath, and gently squeeze out the soapy water. Set it aside while you rinse and refill the dishpan with rinse water, the same temperature as the soapy bath. (Felting can also be caused by sudden changes in temperature.) Lay the skein back in the water and let it rest a few minutes more. Gently squeeze it out once or twice under the water to get rid of the soap and then lift it from the rinse bath. Gently squeeze out the water and roll the skein in a fresh, clean cotton towel to absorb the excess moisture.

Remove the yarn after a while and gently straighten the skein to its original coiled form between your two hands. If the yarn will be used for knitting or crocheting, simply lay the skein on a fresh dry towel (away from sun, wind and pets) and let it dry, turning it occasionally. Drying will take about a day, depending on the climate and weather. Wool can feel dry and still retain up to 30% moisture, so don't go on touch alone—just be a little patient.

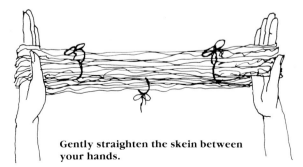

Gently straighten the skein between your hands.

If your yarn is intended for the weft in a weaving, you may want it to dry under tension. Even some knitters and crocheters use this tension method as well, expecially when the skein is hard to untangle because of an excess of twist. Drying the yarn under tension eliminates all or most of the kinks in the yarn, but discourages loft. Slip the top loop of the skein over a hook or pole. Then hang a weight from another hook placed through the bottom loop of the skein (the weight should be just enough to keep the skein straight). The bottom hook can be anything from a shower curtain hook to an S-bent non-rusting wire. The weights can be fishing weights, cans filled with pebbles, or plastic jugs of water. Adjust the weight as needed so that the skein is not overly stretched, but just barely kept straight. Again, keep it away from wind and pets, and out of the sun. (A little sun is okay—after all, the wool grew on the sheep's back!—but ultraviolet light deteriorates all natural fibers and can discolor the wool.)

Spinners with reels sometimes choose to re-reel the wet yarn and let it dry under tension there. This has the advantage of drying the yarn more quickly since the yarn can be spread out on the reel, and drying it under more even tension, since some loops are slightly longer than others in the skein.

Once your yarn is dry, an easy way to store it for later use is in a ball. You can simply place the skein over the back of a chair again (or get a friend to hold the skein between two hands), remove the ties, and begin winding a ball by hand. To wind a ball that pulls from the center (keeping the yarn neat and tidy and the ball stationary), try this method. First start winding a figure-8 between your thumb and little finger. After ten wraps or so, take the figure-8 and fold it in half upon itself, saving out a six- or eight-inch length of yarn from the starting end. Holding the starting end out of the way, pinch the folded figure-8 together with thumb and forefinger, and begin wrapping yarn around both fingers and yarn folds. After about ten wraps or so, remove your fingers, change positions, and begin wrapping. Change positions frequently, and always wrap around two or three fingers *and* the ball of yarn. That keeps your yarn from being wrapped too tightly, which would compress its loft.

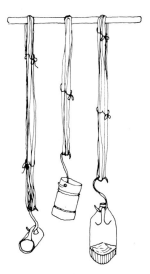

A number of common household items can be used as weights for drying yarn under tension. You will get uniform results if you use objects of similar weight for all the skeins in a batch of yarn.

Begin winding a center-pull ball with a figure-8 around two fingers. Then fold and pinch this center section before you continue to wind.

A clean dry skein can also be stored in its own neat little package. Hold the skein in front of you under a little tension with a thumb through each loop. Rotate your right thumb counterclockwise, so that the skein begins to twist on itself. When the twisted loops are fairly tight around your thumbs, let the skein fold in half, and put one loop through the other. The skein will find its own equilibrium in this twisted state and the secured loop will keep it from coming undone. This is an attractive package that will keep your yarn neat and easy to handle.

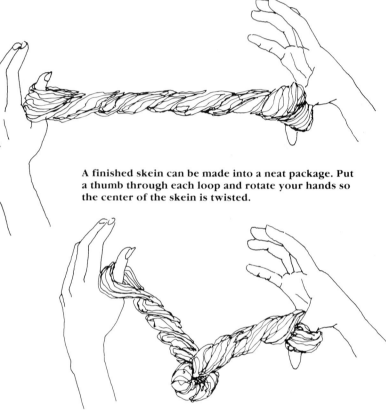

A finished skein can be made into a neat package. Put a thumb through each loop and rotate your hands so the center of the skein is twisted.

Continue until the skein twists back on itself.

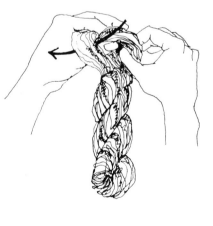

Then tuck one loop through the other.

34

The collection of projects in this book will give you some ideas about how to use your handspun. They use relatively small amounts of yarn and, while they'll benefit from your growing skill, they are tolerant of a new spinner's initial efforts.

An infinitely adjustable HANDSPUN HAT

Designed by Lee Raven

Samples knitted by Linda Ligon and Deborah Robson

This pattern makes a simple ribbed hat, worked in K2, P2 rib in the round, that will fit most adults. After you're familiar with the idea, you can easily adapt it for anyone, large or small. It can be worked with a variety of weights of yarn—the instructions aren't based on a fixed gauge—and only requires between 3 and 3½ ounces of handspun. The yarn can be single or plied. Remember to set the twist before you begin to knit. The hat can be made in one color, or in stripes of natural and/or dyed yarns.

YARN: Start with a two-ply yarn of medium-weight handspun (about as heavy as knitting worsted) or a single strand of bulky handspun. Other sizes will work; you'll base your work on a gauge sample.

NEEDLES: 16-inch circular needle or double-pointed needles, in the size which looks best in your gauge sample.

GAUGE: Variable; determined from swatch. Make a 5 × 5 inch test swatch in stockinette stitch. Try several needle sizes, until you are happy with the look and feel of your sample. Remove your swatch from the needle and measure a 4-inch section. Count the stitches in this section and divide by 4 to get the number of stitches in an inch. This is your gauge. Because handspun is sometimes irregular, measure several times and in several places to find an average number of stitches per inch. If you have a particularly uneven yarn, you may want to make a larger swatch and to measure and count in a larger area.

You can easily adjust this pattern to the exact size of your own handspun and to the size of the future wearer's head. The hat is worked from the brim upwards, so you can test the fit by trying it on as work progresses, or you can compare its size to a favorite hat you already have.

Measure the wearer's head in inches. Subtract between 1½ and 2 inches from this number to get your working circumference (the K2, P2 ribbing is very elastic).

To get the number of stitches to cast on, multiply your gauge by the working circumference. You'll need a number of stitches which is divisible by 4, so add or subtract a couple of stitches if necessary.

Cast on the appropriate number of stitches. Make sure the stitches are not twisted and join the last and first stitches, placing a marker between them so you can keep track of the beginning of the round.

Begin K2, P2 ribbing. For a hat without a turn-up brim, continue for between 5 and 6 inches. For a hat with a turn-up brim, continue for between 9 and 10 inches.

Begin the decrease rounds. *Round 1:* (K2, P2 together), and repeat. (This decreases the P ribs to 1 stitch each.) *Round 2:* (K2, P1), and repeat. Repeat this round for 1 inch. *Round 3:* (K2 together, P1), and repeat. (This decreases the K ribs to 1 stitch each.) *Round 4:* (K1, P1), and repeat. Repeat this round for 1 inch. *Round 5:* (Sl 1, K1, pass sl st over K st), and repeat. Repeat this round until 10-15 stitches remain.

Break the yarn, leaving an 8-inch tail. Thread a yarn needle with this tail and pass it through all the remaining stitches, pulling them together. Secure the yarn (a knot is fine) and weave its tail through the neighboring stitches as invisibly as possible.

These caps can be made from a variety of sizes of yarn. The white one was made from a soft fleece spun by a beginning spinner. The others were made from a commercial dyed rovings, hand carded, and commercially carded wool.

Spinning Wheels

Spindle Wheels

It is believed that the first spinning wheel was an adaptation of the hand spindle. The spindle was turned on its side, and a groove made around the outside of the whorl, making it into a pulley. A string was looped around the whorl or pulley and then around a large **drive wheel.** The large wheel was turned by hand or a simple crank, causing the spindle to rotate. Since the wheel was so much bigger than the whorl, each revolution of the wheel meant many revolutions of the spindle, thus increasing the twisting rate. The spindle could be turned at a constant speed, easily regulated by the spinner. The number of twists in a given yarn length could be adjusted at will, based on the number of revolutions of the wheel, making yarn consistency easier to achieve.

On this early wheel, there was no hook at the tip of the spindle—just a tapered point. The yarn was spiraled to the tip by turning the spindle in the same direction as used for spinning. Because the yarn was held at an angle to the spindle shaft, the last spiral of yarn simply slipped off and then was remade with each revolution of the spindle.

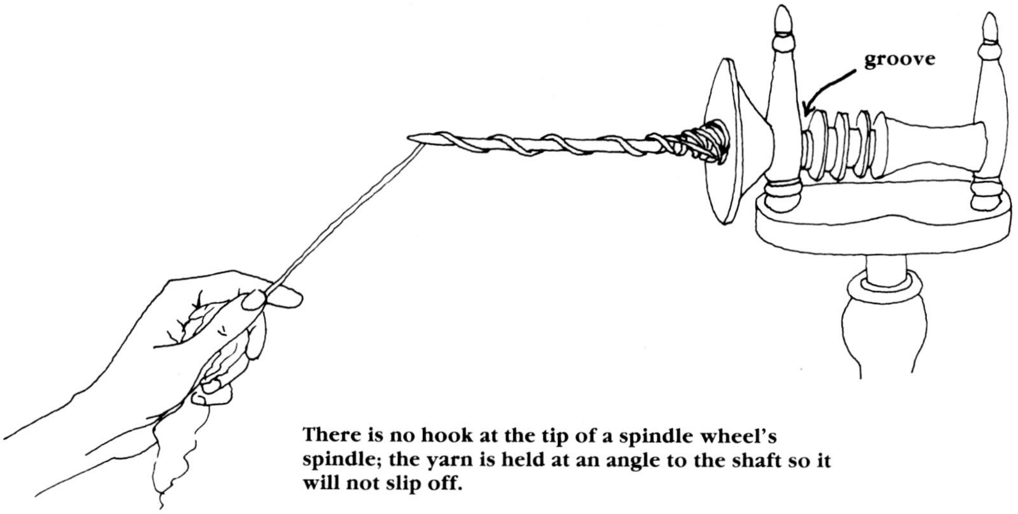

groove

There is no hook at the tip of a spindle wheel's spindle; the yarn is held at an angle to the shaft so it will not slip off.

38

The same place in the yarn would pop gently over the spindle tip with each revolution, each time adding one twist to the length of yarn.

To wind the newly made yarn onto the spindle, the spinner would reverse the direction of the wheel just long enough to unwind the yarn spiraling to the tip, and reverse again to wind on and then spiral the yarn to the tip for the next length of spinning.

You might have seen a "great wheel" (also called a "wool wheel" or "walking wheel") at an antique store, in an attic, or at a demonstration. This is an adaptation of the spindle wheel just described, and was commonly used in this country, Asia and Europe. It continued to be used extensively even after flyer and bobbin wheels were introduced in the sixteenth century. Even the tiny charkha used in India, introduced by Gandhi in this century to spin cotton, is an adaptation of this same wheel design.

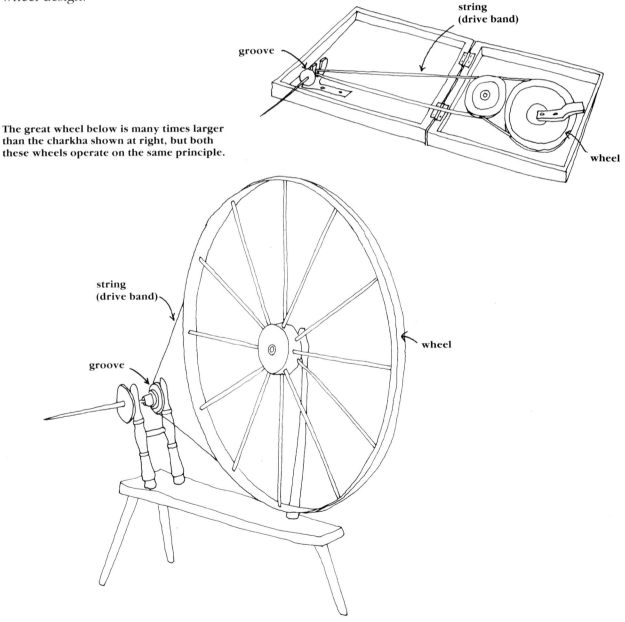

The great wheel below is many times larger than the charkha shown at right, but both these wheels operate on the same principle.

Flyer and Bobbin Wheels

What came next was a wheel that wound the just-spun yarn onto the spindle without the spinner having to break her rhythm. The **flyer and bobbin wheels** did just that, although their mechanisms took a jump in complexity.

If you don't already have a flyer and bobbin wheel to use, see if you can borrow one, or rent one from a spinning and weaving shop. If you can, wait to purchase one until you are more familiar with the choices available (see appendix). Now let's take a brief look at the wheel together before you begin to spin.

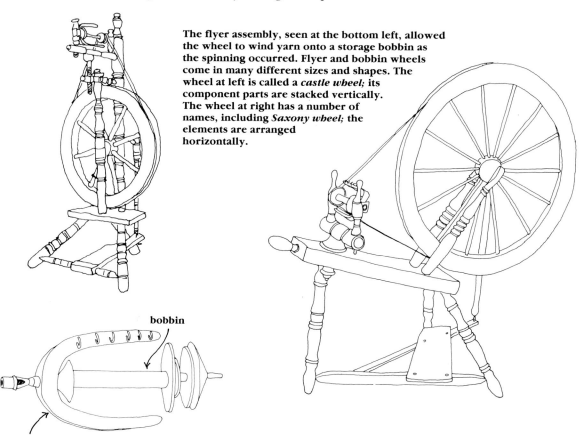

The flyer assembly, seen at the bottom left, allowed the wheel to wind yarn onto a storage bobbin as the spinning occurred. Flyer and bobbin wheels come in many different sizes and shapes. The wheel at left is called a *castle wheel;* its component parts are stacked vertically. The wheel at right has a number of names, including *Saxony wheel;* the elements are arranged horizontally.

bobbin

flyer

As on the spindle wheel, the big drive wheel's job is to turn the spindle, thereby adding twist to the yarn. The spindle looks a bit different now, though—it is a metal shaft with wooden U-shaped "wings"; the wings, or flyer arms, have hooks on them to guide the yarn. Depending on the wheel design, there may or may not be a whorl attached to the shaft as well, either at the bottom of the U or just beyond the tips. This whole assembly of shaft, wings and whorl is known as the **flyer.**

In the spinning devices we've look at previously, the yarn was wound directly onto the spindle shaft. But now a new piece has been added—a **bobbin,** a spool with a hollow core, slipped on over the spindle shaft. The bobbin rotates freely and independently of the shaft, and merely serves to store the yarn. Again, depending on wheel design, there may be a whorl attached to one or both ends of the bobbin.

With this combination of elements a spinner doesn't have to stop after each draft to wind the yarn on. A flyer and bobbin wheel puts a constant, though minor, pull or tension on the yarn. The spinner has control over the amount of tension on the yarn, and can hold the yarn steady and draft as needed, or relax her hold a bit and let the wheel wind the yarn on. In a few moments, we'll take a closer look at that mechanism, but for right now, let's take a look at some other components of the wheel.

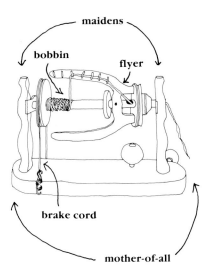

The two pieces that hold up the ends of the flyer shaft are called **maidens.** Usually one of the maidens swings in position to allow you to remove the flyer and change bobbins. When you do change bobbins, you'll have to be sure that you get the maiden aligned correctly before you start again. The unit consisting of the maidens and the flyer and bobbin assembly is known as the **mother-of-all;** on most wheels you can adjust the distance that the mother-of-all sits from the drive wheel.

You may be at a wheel that has the bobbin and flyer assembly to the left and the drive wheel to the right, or the bobbin and flyer may be directly above the drive wheel. In either case, sit in front of the wheel, facing the **treadle,** or foot pedal, with the broad side of the wheel facing you. Use a straight-backed chair that allows your thighs to be supported at right angles to your body. The drive band may or may not be attached—you won't need it just yet, so don't worry about it either way.

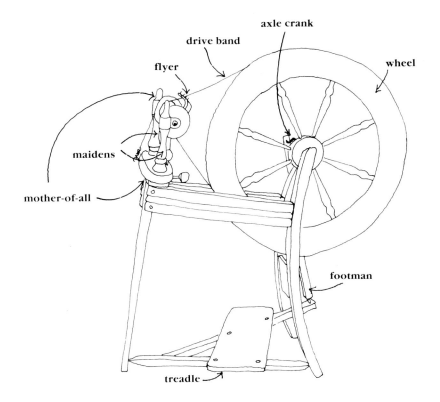

To keep your body in alignment so that your back and shoulders stay comfortable, think about treadling with your right foot and drafting with your left hand. Adjust the position of your chair or wheel until you find a comfortable spot. There is nothing wrong with treadling with both feet for a while when you tire or need to change positions slightly; you can even use your left foot if it doesn't twist your body too much. But try always to be comfortable, relaxed, and with your shoulders and body pretty much square to the wheel. Don't sit in a soft chair, or one that is too low or too high, or your legs will tire quickly. Your thighs should be parallel with the floor, or perhaps angled slightly downward toward the knees.

With your hand on the rim near the top of the wheel (over the drive band if there is one), give the wheel a push in the clockwise direction (top of the wheel rotating to the right). Or you can hook a finger over a spoke near the rim to get the wheel going. With your right foot lightly on the treadle, wait until the treadle just passes the peak of its travel, then press it down with the ball of your foot to drive the wheel around again. The **footman** is the piece that connects the treadle to the **axle crank** of the wheel. Notice that as the treadle reaches its peak of travel, the crank is just coming over the top of its rotation; it is at that point that you want to treadle again. Bring the wheel gradually up to speed in this manner until you are treadling about once a second or so.

There is one more adjustment to make before you start spinning. If you have a single drive wheel, there will be some sort of **brake cord** or **brake band**. On some wheels, like the Louet, the flyer has a brake made of a leather strap over the front of the flyer shaft. It is adjustable by a screw mechanism. Leave the tension very loose for now. On other wheels, like the Ashford, the brake will be a separate cord that goes over the groove in the rim of the bobbin. It will have a spring at one end and a turning peg at the other. Adjust the brake band so that there is a slight amount of tension put on the spring.

Look at the end of the flyer shaft facing you. There is a hole there, called the **orifice.** Near the orifice is a hole leading out of the side of the flyer shaft, called the **eye.** As you are spinning, your yarn will travel into the orifice, out of the side of the shaft through the eye, up and over the hooks along one wing of the flyer, and onto the bobbin. (Some small wheels have no orifice or eye, but just a large hook attached to the front end of the flyer.)

As the wheel goes faster, you'll find it's a little easier to control. But you'll also need to practice going very slow. When you actually start spinning on this wheel, things will seem to happen very fast, and you'll naturally want to start out with slow treadling until you get the feel of things. But there is a price for slower treadling—the slower you go, the greater chance that the wheel won't quite make it around, that it will reverse direction on you and begin to unwind your yarn. So you want to gain good control with your foot now at a variety of speeds, especially the slower ones, always maintaining the clockwise direction of the wheel (for a Z-twist yarn). Most of your attention will be taken up with drafting and controlling twist, and winding on, so if your foot can work automatically, so much the better.

Let's get the **drive band** or **drive cord** on. Supplied with your wheel should be a circular cotton cord (sometimes plastic) that will travel in the groove around the rim of the big drive wheel to a flyer or bobbin whorl (sometimes called a **pulley**). We need to stop and take note here, though, of the kind of wheel that you have, so you can place the cord properly.

Wheel Types

There are three popular types of flyer and bobbin wheels: 1) the **single drive, bobbin lead** (a single drive band goes from the drive wheel to the bobbin whorl—the bobbin is the driven element, and goes faster than, or leads, the flyer); 2) a **single drive, flyer lead** (a single drive band goes from the drive wheel to the flyer whorl, driving the flyer which leads the bobbin); and 3) the **double drive** (a doubled drive band goes around the drive wheel with one loop encircling the flyer whorl, and the other loop encircling the bobbin whorl, driving both elements).

If there is no whorl on the flyer, but there is one on the bobbin, then you have a single drive, bobbin lead wheel. One of the most popular brands of wheel with this type of mechanism is the Louet. Put the drive band on so it goes around the rim of the wheel and around the largest whorl (if there is more than one) on the bobbin.

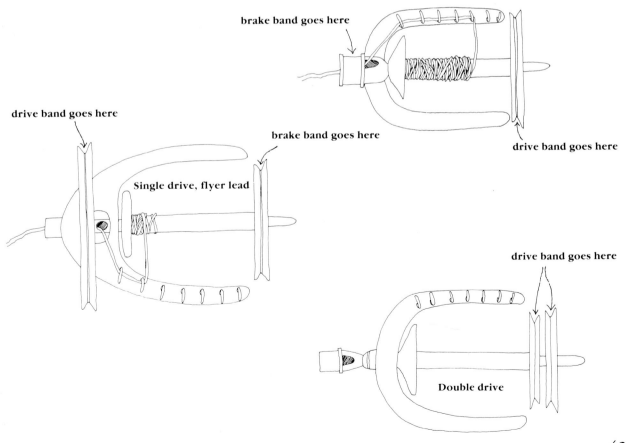

Single drive, bobbin lead

brake band goes here

drive band goes here

drive band goes here

drive band goes here

brake band goes here

Single drive, flyer lead

drive band goes here

Double drive

If there is no whorl on the bobbin, but there is one on the flyer, then you have a single drive, flyer lead wheel (the bobbin will have a groove in one rim). Ashford is a very popular brand with this type of mechanism. Put the drive band around the drive wheel rim, and around the largest whorl (if there is more than one) on the flyer.

If there is a whorl on the bobbin *and* on the shaft beyond the wing tips of the flyer, then you have a double drive wheel. Make a doubled circle of the drive band, put it around the drive wheel, and then loop one end around the largest flyer whorl and one end around the bobbin whorl.

On most wheels (the Louet is an exception) there is an adjustment you can make to the drive band tension. Look for a knob that when turned will allow you to move the whole flyer and bobbin assembly toward or away from the drive wheel. Adjust the position of the flyer and bobbin assembly so that when you push down on the drive cord with your finger, it moves about an inch and a half. That's a good tension to start with, though you may want to adjust it later.

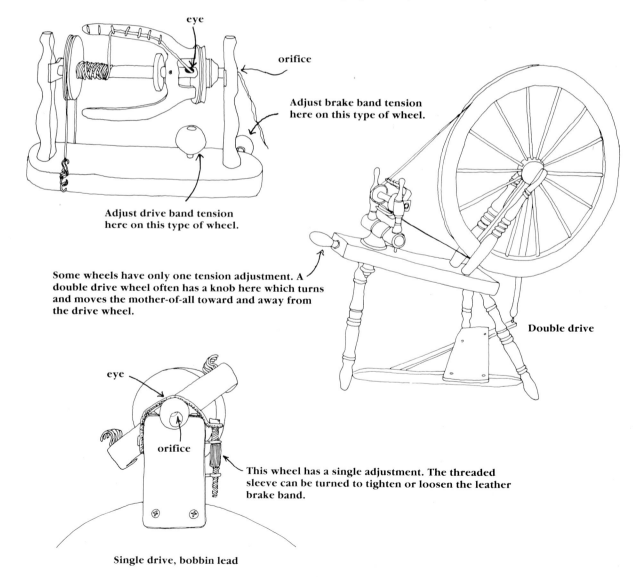

Single drive, flyer lead

eye

orifice

Adjust brake band tension here on this type of wheel.

Adjust drive band tension here on this type of wheel.

Some wheels have only one tension adjustment. A double drive wheel often has a knob here which turns and moves the mother-of-all toward and away from the drive wheel.

Double drive

eye

orifice

This wheel has a single adjustment. The threaded sleeve can be turned to tighten or loosen the leather brake band.

Single drive, bobbin lead

Spinning on the Wheel

To start spinning, you'll need a starter yarn or leader about two feet long. Finger-spin a length of Z-twist yarn, or take a length from your hand spindle. Tie one end securely around the core of the bobbin—it must stay in one place and not slip around as the bobbin turns. Take the leader up and over the hook nearest to where you've tied it, and over all the succeeding hooks between there and the eye of the flyer. Thread the yarn through the eye and out the orifice. Some wheels are equipped with a separate yarn hook to help with this threading. You can make one out of a straightened paper clip, too; find a way to attach it to your wheel, for you'll use it often.

You're ready to spin. Take some of your teased wool, or some commercially carded wool, in your left hand, and make a join with the leader. When you are ready to add twist, get the wheel going with your right hand, and then take over treadling with your foot. Complete your join and begin spinning a length of yarn. Draft with your left hand, keeping the right hand about 12″ from the orifice and using it only to help draft any difficult fibers by tugging on the yarn.

As you spin, you should feel a constant but gentle pull on your yarn from the wheel. As you draft it should be easy to keep the yarn from winding on; there shouldn't be so much **take-up** or **wind-on** tension that the yarn is yanked from your grasp and sucked into the wheel. When you allow the wheel to pull the yarn in, it should do so readily. If the take-up on your wheel is too light, too much twist will be added to your yarn before it is wound on, or it might not wind on at all. If the take-up is too heavy, the yarn is likely to slip out of your hands or break and zip into the orifice.

Adjusting Take-Up Tension

The whole trick to winding-on with flyer and bobbin wheels is to make the flyer and bobbin turn at different rates. During drafting, when you're not allowing the yarn to wind on, the flyer and bobbin turn at the same speed. But when you relax your hold on the yarn, one element, either the flyer or the bobbin, slows down, allowing wind-on to occur. On single drive, bobbin lead wheels, it is the bobbin that leads, winding the yarn on as the flyer slows. On single drive, flyer lead wheels, the flyer leads, winding the yarn around the slower bobbin. On double drive wheels, the bobbin again leads, winding the yarn on as the flyer slows.

You'll need to attach a leader to your bobbin before you start to spin. Tie it securely around the bobbin core, lead it up over the hooks, and thread it through the eye and the orifice.

45

To adjust your take-up tension on single drive wheels, increase or decrease the *brake* band friction on the flyer or the bobbin; the greater the braking friction, the greater the take-up tension. On double drive wheels, there are two things that you can do: 1) move the drive band to another flyer whorl (the greater the difference in size between the flyer and bobbin whorls the greater the take-up), or 2) increase or decrease the *drive* band tension; the greater the drive band tension, the greater the take-up tension. Adjust your take-up as necessary so that it feels like a comfortable regular pull as you draft, and so that an arm's length of yarn takes no more than about two treadles to wind-on.

Drafting Methods

There are two methods of spinning that you may recognize from other spinners that you have observed. In one, the spinner pulls the fiber supply away from the wheel as the twist advances and forms the yarn. An arm's length is spun, and then wound on all at once (except for the last six inches or so, which serve as the starter length for the next draft). This method is similar to the draft you used with the supported spindle or the spindle wheel—essentially a one-handed draft—and can be referred to as the **long draw.** It can be speeded up considerably with practice, and results in a relatively even yarn.

In the other method, the yarn is "pulled" from the stationary fiber supply with the free hand, a few inches at a time, and fed into the wheel simultaneously with each pull. This is more like the method you used with the drop spindle, and is often referred to by spinners as the **short draw,** the **inchworm** or the **push-pull** method. It can be moderately speeded up with practice, though less so than the long draw, and results in a slightly more textured yarn. (It is more difficult with this method to feed a constant number of fibers into the drafting zone.)

Spinners often like to start out with the short draw technique until they gain some confidence and control, and then move on to the long draw. I encourage you to become familiar with both, and later on with other techniques that we'll discuss. There are a number of drafting methods possible, and the more you are familiar with, the easier time you'll have adjusting to different fiber types and tools.

Spinning Hints

Work to gain better and better control over what is happening in the drafting zone. Become familiar with what happens inside the triangle, and then what results in the texture of the yarn. Draft well in front of the twist so that drafting is smooth and easy, not hard or jerky. Keep the fiber supply hand gently holding the fibers an inch or two behind the drafting fibers—you'll still be able to feel the fibers slipping through the fiber mass. Stop every now and again to test the soundness of your yarn. If you're doing the long draw, a little more twist will be added to your length of yarn as you are winding on, so if it has just about enough twist, go ahead and let it wind on.

When you let up on the tension to wind the yarn on, keep the yarn just taut. If you let go too quickly, the yarn can tangle on itself or around the flyer. Just follow the yarn in at the speed the wheel wants to take it.

When you have wound on a few lengths of yarn, stop the wheel and see where your yarn is stored. Move the yarn over one hook so it will begin building up in another spot. With an eye toward getting your yarn off smoothly later, fill up the bobbin as evenly as you can, never letting it build up into a big mound in one place where it can fall over and tangle. A good practice is to march the yarn from front to back, hook by hook, and then from back to front, repeating until the bobbin is about three-fourths full.

How much twist should you be putting in? Well, enough so that your yarn holds together, so that it is sound, but not so much that it tangles and wraps on itself before you can get it wound on the bobbin. A good test is to stop after you have spun a length of yarn, move your two hands together allowing the yarn to twist back on itself, and have a look. Would you knit with that two-ply yarn, or perhaps use it in a weaving? If it looks good to you, and it's neither pulling apart nor harsh with tangles, it's fine.

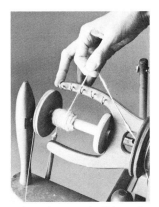

When the yarn builds up in one area of the bobbin, stop and move it over one hook.

In the long draw, you pull the fiber supply away from the wheel as the twist advances. This is essentially a one-handed technique. Your free hand can assist, as it did when you were spinning on the drop spindle, by plucking seeds from the yarn or by occasionally pinching off the twist so your active hand can readjust the fiber supply. With well-prepared fibers and some experience, this is a fast and smooth spinning method.

In the short draw, the fiber supply stays in one place and you "pull" bits of fiber toward the wheel. The twist catches them and makes the yarn. As you begin to spin, you may feel more control with this technique.

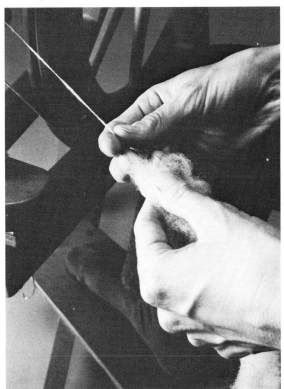

Problems With Your Flyer and Bobbin Wheel Spinning

1. The yarn doesn't take up, won't wind on.
First of all, remember that the flyer and bobbin have to travel at different speeds for wind-on to take place. On single drive wheels, be sure the brake band has enough tension to slow the bobbin or flyer as needed.

On double drive wheels, be sure that one loop of the drive band is on a flyer whorl, and the other on the bobbin whorl. It is easy to inadvertently put a loop on each of the flyer whorls, or both on the bobbin whorl, and in that case, no wind-on can take place. Check that the drive band has enough tension on it to turn both flyer and bobbin, and is not just slipping around the whorls.

After you've checked the drive and brake bands, look closely at the yarn traveling over the hooks. Sometimes the yarn, or a tangle of fibers, can get looped around a hook and get caught there. Or sometimes the yarn has come off the hooks completely. Check also that the yarn didn't get wrapped around the flyer shaft, which can happen if you try to wind the yarn on too quickly.

If you're just starting a bobbin, it may be that your leader yarn is not secured around the bobbin, and is slipping instead of pulling on the yarn. Tighten the knot, or simply turn the bobbin by hand to wind several layers of the leader tightly over the knot.

It is possible that your yarn is too thick to pass through the orifice and eye of the flyer. Check the entire path the yarn takes to see if it is getting caught up in one particular spot.

2. Too much take-up.
If you are working with a single drive wheel, loosen the brake band on either the flyer or bobbin as needed, until the take-up is just as you need it.

On double drive wheels, put the drive band on one of the flyer whorls with a smaller diameter for reduced take-up. You can also try loosening the drive band tension.

With any of these solutions, you are, in effect, decreasing the differential in speed between the flyer and bobbin, thus reducing take-up.

3. Drive wheel is hard to treadle.
All the moving parts of this wheel need to be lubricated to move smoothly and efficiently. Be sure the wheel axle and the treadle pivots are well oiled. Oil the flyer shaft at both ends of the bobbin, too, and at the extreme ends where they rest on the bearings. (See pages 113-14.)

The greater the tension you put on the drive band, the harder you have to work to turn the wheel. Adjust your drive band tension to be as loose as you can while still maintaining good wheel performance.

Make sure that the bobbin can rotate freely on the flyer shaft and that the flyer can rotate freely on its bearings.

4. Too little twist going into the yarn.

Slow down your drafting just a bit, and speed up your treadling just a bit, so that more twist enters the yarn.

Decrease the take-up tension so that the yarn will wind on slower. If the wheel pulls the yarn out of your hand too fast, you won't be getting enough twist as you draft, and you may end up losing the end of the yarn into the orifice.

5. Too much twist going into the yarn.

Speed up your drafting just a bit, and slow your treadling, so that less twist enters the yarn.

Increase your take-up tension so that less twist enters the yarn during wind-on.

6. Losing your end.

If the wheel seems to grab the end and you lose it through the orifice, stop the wheel, find the end on the bobbin, rethread the end through the orifice, make a join, and continue spinning. Occasionally the end can be hard to find, especially if it was pulled in under a great deal of tension and got buried under the layers of yarn, or if it got so thin before it broke that it seems to disappear. In that case, try using a piece of masking tape to fish it out. It will also help greatly if you keep track of which hook you were on, so you know where to search.

7. "Throwing" the drive band.

If the drive band comes off the main wheel while you are spinning, it is because the groove in the main wheel does not line up properly with the groove in the flyer or bobbin whorl. Be sure that the maidens are aligned properly, and that the flyer and bobbin can each rotate freely. Unfortunately, some wheels are not made as well as others, and a thrown drive band can be a chronic problem.

8. Just can't get everything going at once.

Don't worry about it a bit. You can't focus your concentration on everything you've learned, and your hands and feet have all been given very different tasks.

If you have a friend who can help you, break up the tasks by having one person control the wheel, and the other person control the yarn (treadler sits, spinner stands). Don't switch places until you each feel comfortable with the timing and actions.

If you don't have someone around to help, all you have to do is back up a bit and remind your hands and foot once again of what they need to do. Practice treadling without spinning until your attention can wander freely. Practice spinning on the supported or drop spindle until the drafting feels more controlled and comfortable. Make sure the drive band has about an inch and a half of play in it (when you push it down with a forefinger), and that the brake band is just tight enough to wind the yarn on, and no tighter. Treadling should be easy, almost leisurely, and the yarn should stay in your hands when you want it to.

You'll have better control, and more time, if you work farther from the orifice. Don't let the drafting zone approach any closer than a foot from the wheel, and work even farther back if you can. This will give you time to see and appraise the yarn length you are working on and to make any adjustments in your drafting or treadling before it disappears onto the bobbin.

Putting It All Together

Take a deep breath, relax your shoulders and neck, and sit back in your chair. It is not at all uncommon to see spinners hunched over their wheels in concentrated effort, but it is not a position that can be maintained comfortably very long, and it doesn't enhance the smoothly flowing rhythms of spinning good yarns. In order to sit comfortably at your wheel for stretches of time, you need to make yourself relax your neck, shoulders, back, and thighs as much as possible. You will find that the more you are able to relax, the easier spinning rhythmically will become. And the more easily and rhythmically you spin, the more and better yarn you can produce.

As you spin, especially in the beginning, you may notice that gradually your shoulders, neck and back may tense back up as you work. You may tend to lean forward and over your work. Just be

The position in which you spin will affect both your stamina and the yarn you make. Relax—especially in your shoulders, neck and back—and remember to breathe easily.

It's tempting to sit closer to the wheel and to try to spin right next to the orifice, but it's not productive. If you find yourself in this position, relax and sit back— or take a short break.

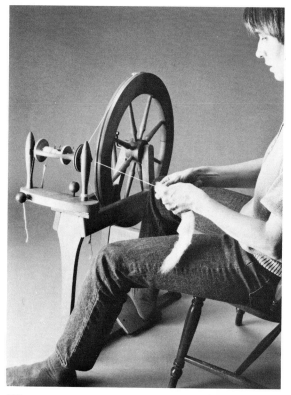

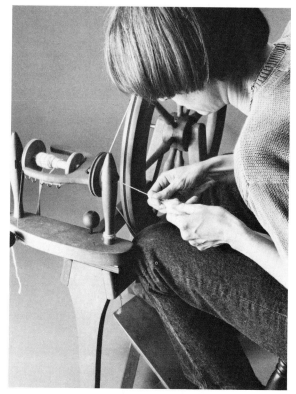

conscious of this happening and make an effort to relax again. Work in a well lighted and ventilated place, in a comfortable, but not soft, chair. Reorient yourself to the wheel so that drafting does not cause you to twist your back. You do not have to sit exactly square to the wheel, but rather in a position that will allow you to work comfortably.

If you're having trouble seeing your yarn clearly, try putting a contrasting background behind it, on your lap or on the floor. Black yarn against a white cloth or white yarn against a black cloth is much easier to see.

Once you've spun a bobbin or two of wool, you should start to feel more comfortable with the rhythms of drafting and treadling. You may notice that you can speed up your actions a bit, and at the same time, that your yarns are less likely to break or snarl. New spinners often say that there is a threshold to be crossed: in the beginning, nothing seems to work—least of all your hands—and then suddenly, everything begins to fall into place, as you get a "feel" for the new actions. That same feeling of initial clumsiness followed by a satisfying jump in dexterity is common to most learned physical activities, so if you feel awkward for a while in the beginning, remind yourself that we've all been there, and that a fine reward is waiting just around the corner.

As you become more comfortable with what's happening at your hands, you may also notice something happening at the wheel: as the bobbin fills, the take-up tension gradually decreases, until the wheel is no longer pulling in the yarn at the comfortable rate you started out with. By the time the bobbin is three-fourths full, this slower rate of wind-on may feel suddenly quite noticeable. If you keep spinning without making an adjustment, not only will the rhythm of your spinning be disturbed, but even more importantly, each length of yarn will become slightly more twisted than the last, as you wait longer and longer for each length to wind on. Now, some differences in the amount of twist in your yarn are fine, and to be expected, especially in the beginning. But gross differences will affect how your yarn, and thus your finished garment, will look and behave. By the time you reach a nearly full bobbin, differences in twist amounts can become pronounced.

As the diameter of the bobbin increases, then, take-up tension will need to be increased as well, in order for you to get the same rate of wind-on (and twist) that you got nearer the beginning. You can just reach over and make a small adjustment to the brake band (single drive) or drive band (double drive) until the take-up tension feels right again. That will work for a short while. It turns out, though, that after you reach that three-fourths-full point, you have to adjust the tension more and more often, because the wheel is working less and less efficiently. Rather than forcing the bobbin to fill to capacity, it's better just to plan on filling your bobbins to about three-fourth or seven-eighths full. Then change to a new bobbin, or wind off your yarn.

Changing to a New Bobbin

In order to switch to an empty bobbin, you must first remove the flyer. On most wheels, one of the support posts (maidens) for the flyer will turn in place so that the flyer can be removed. You may need to loosen the drive or brake band on your wheel, but in any case, slip the drive and brake bands off the flyer and bobbin as you remove them from the wheel. Then just slip the full bobbin off the flyer shaft, and slip the empty bobbin on. If the ends of the bobbin are of two different sizes, be sure and put the smaller end toward the base of the flyer, and the larger end toward the tips of the flyer. Put the flyer and bobbin unit back in place, along with the drive and brake bands. Be sure that you line up the **bearings** (the leather, metal, or plastic surfaces on the maidens that support the flyer shaft) exactly perpendicular to the flyer shaft, so that the shaft can rotate freely.

On double drive wheels, you'll need to remove the flyer whorl before you can remove the bobbin (on some wheels the flyer whorl has reverse threads—just unscrew it in the other direction). Don't forget to put the flyer whorl back on after you've changed bobbins, and to place the drive band so that one loop is on the bobbin whorl and one loop is on a flyer whorl.

On wheels with a hook in place of the orifice and eye, you'll need to hold the flyer whorl steady while you unscrew the flyer from the wheel.

Whenever you change bobbins, take the opportunity to oil the shaft where the bobbin will ride, and both ends of the flyer shaft where it rests in its bearings. A well-oiled wheel runs noiselessly and effortlessly.

When you change bobbins on any wheel, remember to slip the drive band and the brake back into position in the pulley grooves before you replace the flyer assembly.

Changing the bobbin on this type of wheel requires that you rotate the front maiden (old style) or pop the flyer shaft out of a slot in the bearing on the back maiden (new style) before you remove the flyer assembly. The bobbin slides off the shaft and can be replaced with another bobbin.

To change the bobbin on this type of wheel, begin by slipping the drive band off the far end of the bobbin. Then loosen the leather brake band and slip it off the end of the flyer assembly, as shown. When you are learning to spin, put the bobbin on the shaft with its small end toward you. Later on you can reverse it—the wheel will spin faster!

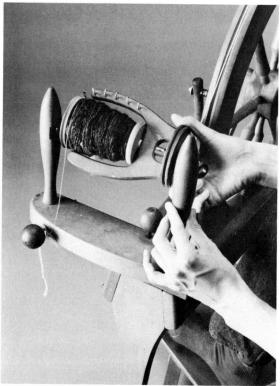

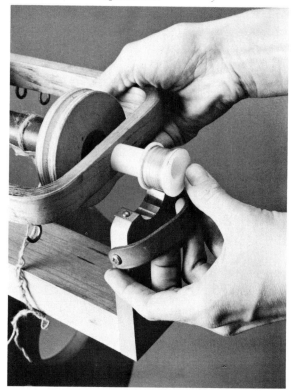

Winding Off Your Yarn

You can leave your full bobbin on the wheel and wind your yarn off directly from there if you like. Pull the yarn off from the side of the bobbin rather than through the orifice. Loosen or remove any brake or drive band that will hinder the bobbin from turning. Get your niddy noddy, or a reel, wind your yarn onto it, and make a skein. Some spinners like to position the niddy noddy or the reed across the room from the wheel; if the yarn is freshly spun, and is kept fairly taut while winding off, this practice helps to even out the amount of twist in the yarn length between wheel and reel.

If the bobbin turns too fast, it will often over-rotate and begin to wind the yarn up in the other direction. When you tug again on the yarn to continue your winding off, the bobbin will begin to rotate, but then must suddenly stop and change direction to continue unwinding the yarn in the original direction. This sudden snapping tension on your yarn may cause it to break. The remedy is just to slow the bobbin's free rotation a bit by putting on a very lightly tensioned brake band or drive cord.

Make a skein of your yarn complete with figure-8 ties, and set the twist by whichever method you prefer. When dry, store the skein in its own twisted package or in a ball.

You can also store your full bobbins on a *lazy kate* (see page 80). Later you can make skeins or spin plied yarns directly from the bobbins.

Leave your full bobbin on the wheel when you wind off. Pull the yarn directly from the side of the bobbin, and use the brake as a tensioner.

On a double drive wheel, slide the flyer assembly out of the bearings on the maidens. The maidens sometimes rotate.

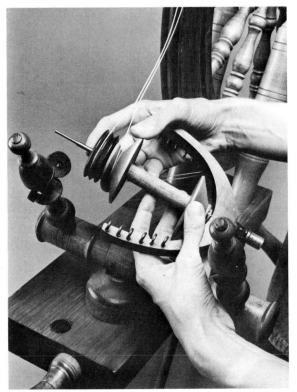

Then unscrew the pulley from the end of the flyer shaft. You can now remove and replace the bobbin.

Great socks! They also make sense of small amounts of leftover yarn. Although these were worked in a singles yarn, two-ply can also be used.

THREE-SEASON SOCKS

Designed by Margaret Boyd

You can use odd lots of dyed, blended, or unusual yarns in these great wool socks, suitable for fall, winter, and spring, or you can spin yarn especially for them. You'll need to spin a fairly consistent size—comparable to a commercial sport weight—to make them work. They're just right for wearing under boots or around the house. Once you're familiar with the pattern, you can adapt it to different weights of yarn.

YARN: Approximately 250 to 300 yards (about 6 ounces) of handspun wool singles at about 880 yards per pound. This was spun from Corriedale fleece—nice and soft, but still able to withstand some wear—with a 3- to 3½-inch staple.

The raw wool was soaked in warm sudsy water, dyed with natural dyes, and dried. Then it was hand carded; the colors were blended for a tweedy effect on the unstriped socks.

The spun yarn was washed, rinsed, and hung weighted to dry.

NEEDLES: Double-pointed needles, sizes 4 and 2 or the sizes required to obtain the correct gauge with your yarn.

GAUGE: Make and check a gauge swatch as described on page 36. On the larger needles, 6 stitches = 1 inch, 8 rows = 1 inch. These socks are about 9 inches in circumference at the top; the ribbing stretches to fit a calf size of 12 to 14 inches. If you want larger socks, cast on additional stitches in multiples of 4.

Ribbing: With larger needles, cast on 44 stitches. Work in K2, P2 ribbing, dividing stitches equally between 3 of 4 double-pointed needles and working with the fourth. Rib for 3½ inches. (Finished height

of sock from ankle bone will be 8 inches; if you want a higher sock, knit more here.) Change to smaller needles. Continue with K2, P2 ribbing for 2½ inches more. Change to larger needles and work 2 inches in stockinette stitch.

Heel: *Divide stitches.* Knit first 11 stitches (plus one for each multiple of 4 you added) onto first instep needle; the same number onto the second instep needle; and twice that number onto the third (heel) needle. Work only heel stitches for 10 rows, in stockinette stitch, slipping the first stitch of each row. End with a knit row. *Turn heel.* Continue to work only heel stitches. Slip 1, P to 3 stitches past center of heel, P2 together, and turn. Slip 1, K8, K2 together, turn. Continue, always working one more stitch on each row before the decrease until all stitches have been worked. K 1 row, P 1 row.

Instep: *Divide stitches.* Knit half of heel stitches and slip to spare needle. Knit remaining half, then pick up and knit 8 stitches along side of heel. With second needle, knit across stitches on 2 instep needles. With third needle, pick up and knit 8 stitches along other side of heel; then knit onto this needle the stitches slipped onto

the spare needle. Now slip 2 stitches from each end of the instep needle onto each of the two side-and-heel needles. **Shape instep.** *Round 1:* On first needle, K to 3 stitches from the end, K2 together, K1. K across instep needle. On third needle, K1, slip 1 stitch as if to knit, K1, pass the slip stitch over final K stitch. *Round 2:* Repeat round 1. *Round 3:* Knit around. Repeat these three rounds three more times.

Foot: Work even until sock measures 2½ inches from beginning of instep. If the length of your sock (from ankle bone to toe) will be more than 9 inches, add the difference at this point. Then switch to the smaller needles and work even for 3 inches.

Toe: Knit 1 round. *Decrease round:* On first needle, K to 3 stitches from the end, K2 together, K1. On second needle, K1, slip 1, K1, pass slip stitch over; knit to within 3 stitches of end, K 2 together, K1. On third needle, K1, slip 1, K1, pass slip stitch over; knit to end of needle. Repeat decrease round until 10 stitches remain. Bind off and stitch opening closed.

Fiber Preparations

There are a number of ways in which fibers can be prepared for spinning, some of them quite simple, some very involved. The aim of preparation is to make the fibers suitable for drafting with the degree of control you want. The more careful and thorough the preparation, the more control you have over the size and texture of the yarn. Fibers that are prepared very little or not at all will dictate to a large degree the type of yarn that you can spin.

Fiber preparations fall into two major categories: *carded* and *combed.* These terms are used to describe not only wool preparations, but those of cotton, silks, and other fibers as well. The types of preparation affect the kind of yarn that can be spun, so it is important to become familiar with them.

Carded fibers result in **woolen** yarns: soft, lofty, fuzzy yarns containing many fiber lengths. The fibers are first washed and dried, and then brushed over opposing sets of short wire teeth to open and separate the fibers into a uniform mass.

Carded preparations from the mills are called **slivers, batts,** or **rovings,** depending on how they look when they come off the machine. Slivers *(sly·* vers) are thick, long, continuous strands of carded wool. They contain no twist. Slivers need no further preparation and can be spun directly from the end. Batts are thick cushiony rectangles made of a succession of thin layers of carded wool. They can be separated into strips or layers for spinning, or they can be used for felting or padding. Rovings *(row·* vings) are very similar to slivers, but they are much thinner, and contain a slight amount of twist. A **pencil roving** is about as thick as a pencil, and is usually spun without further drafting.

Carded preparations that you make at home are called batts or **rolags** *(roll·* lags). Batts are made on small tabletop carding machines usually cranked by hand. Batts are small, and must be put through the machine several times for the wool to be uniformly separated. Rolags are made with a set of **hand carders** (two paddle boards faced with closely set rows of fine wire teeth). The fibers are brushed and opened with the carders and then rolled into big cigar shapes of fluffy wool.

Combed fibers result in **worsted** yarns: strong, smooth, shiny yarns that contain only long fibers. In the mills, the fibers go first through the carding process to open them up, and then are combed so that the short or broken fibers are removed and the remaining long fibers are left lying parallel to one another. Combing is done at home with the aid of a pair of **wool combs.** Each comb has rows of long sharpened tines which are used to separate and align the fibers, removing short fibers and tangles in the process. Whether they are formed at the mill or at home, combed preparations are called **tops.**

The Carding Process

You'll be able to find hand carders in spinning and weaving shops, or by mail order from one of the fiber magazines. You'll often be given a choice between straight-backed carders or curved-back carders, and between wool carders or cotton carders. For your first pair, I suggest that you get curved-back wool carders. The curved backs will give you more precise control during the carding process, and the wool carders (also called wool cards) handle a wide range of fiber types and diameters. Later on, when you want to experiment with carding and blending the short delicate fibers like cotton, some of the silks, cashmere, and Angora rabbit, you'll want to invest in cotton carders with their finer and more closely set teeth.

The purpose of hand carding is to open, separate, and straighten the wool fibers. The product is a small batt or rolag of open lofty wool,

This is all wool! It has been prepared for spinning in a number of different ways. There are (1) rolags, (2) a carded batt, (3) roving, (4) pencil roving, (5) sliver, and (6) tops. The tools at lower left are hand carders, which are used to make rolags.

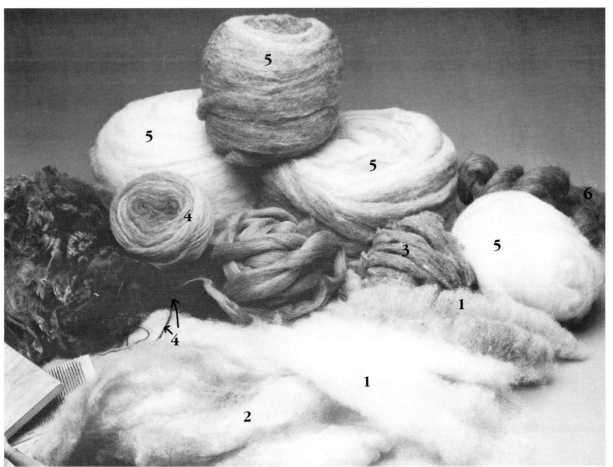

Straight-back wool carders

Curved back cotton carders

which makes your drafting much easier, and gives you greater control in spinning the woolen yarn you desire. Woolen yarns are warm and insulative because of the trapped air among the fibers; they are fuzzier at the surface than worsted yarns, and are generally softer and loftier. Woolen yarns are excellent for knitting and crocheting, and as the weft yarns in weaving.

The instructions that follow are broken down in stages so that you can easily follow the directions as well as the reasoning for each action. You'll find when you get a bit of practice under your belt, though, that these stages will all meld neatly and smoothly together into a single process. In stage one, you'll put some wool on a carder. In stage two you'll brush it gently while the fibers gradually transfer from the first to the second carder. In stage three you'll complete the transfer of wool using some slightly different motions. Stage four is a repetition of stages two and three until all the fibers are equally opened and brushed. In stage five, you'll remove the wool from the carders and form it into a rolag, ready for spinning.

The first thing to do is **charge** a carder with wool. Take one of the carders in your left hand, palm up, with the handle pointing away from you and the wooden back resting against your leg (wire teeth pointing up). This left hand carder will remain stationary while the other carder does the work. Take a little clean wool in your right hand and begin pulling it across the teeth of the carder from the handle end toward the front end, so that the fibers are just held by the teeth. Load it just until

Charge the carder by taking a handful of wool and pulling it across the teeth of the carder. Do this gently; brush the wool across the teeth and let them grab part of it. Repeat until you have a thin, even layer of wool across the carder.

Begin to card by taking the other carder in your right hand. Use a light, rocking motion. The tips of the teeth on the carders should barely meet.

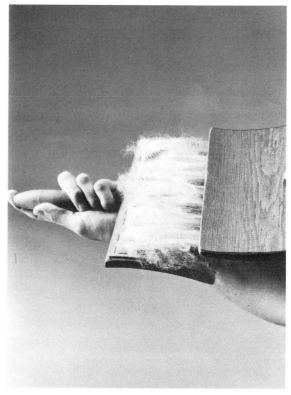

58

the teeth are barely obscured—you can card a thin layer more efficiently and evenly than a thick layer. Fiber ends should extend beyond the front edge of the carder, but should not extend beyond the teeth at the handle end.

Now take the other carder in your right hand, palm down, with the handle toward you and the wood back uppermost. You are going to brush the wool on the left carder with the right carder, using a gentle rocking motion, so that the teeth at the handle end of the right carder engage the wool first, and as you rock through and brush back, the front teeth engage the wool last.

Here's how to begin. Starting with the teeth near the handle of the right carder, begin to stroke through the tips of the wool that extend beyond the front edge of the left carder. Stroke down, back and through as you rock the carder forward. With this first stroke, the teeth of the carders shouldn't even meet. On the next stroke, move the carders a little closer together to pick up the extending fiber tips again. Follow through with your rocking stroke, but notice that the teeth of the carders will overlap by about an inch or so this time. When you get to the point in your stroke where the teeth meet, avoid pulling *down* and through so that the teeth interlock and end up scraping past one another. Instead, just pull *back* and through so that the teeth barely touch as they pass.

On your successive strokes, as the carders overlap more and more, continue the rocking motion as you brush the wool. Brush the wool on

When your wool appears to be evenly divided between the cards, you will lift and transfer the remaining fibers on the left carder to the right carder. The rocking motion of your hands will be emphasized over the brushing motion.

With each stroke, overlap your carders more. When you complete this step, all the fibers should be on your right carder.

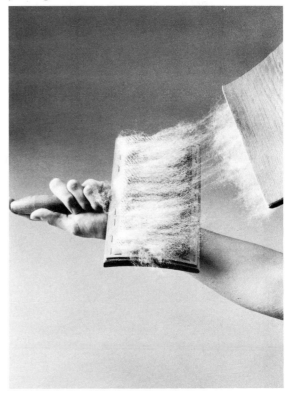

top of the teeth, not the wool imbedded *in* the teeth. If you mesh the teeth of the carders together and forcefully pull them past one another, you will end up tearing and breaking the delicate fibers, and putting excessive wear on your carders.

You will notice throughout this process (it will take about five to ten strokes) that wool has been transferring from the left carder onto the right carder. When all the wool on top of the teeth has been carded, and both carders look equally charged, it is time to start *lifting* and brushing the remaining fibers from the teeth of the left carder, as they transfer to the right carder. At this stage, the rocking motion is particularly emphasized, and the brushing-back motion, a little de-emphasized.

Here's how to go about it. Starting at the front edge, engage the fiber tips hanging off the front end of the left carder as before, but do not stroke back. Instead, rock the right carder forward, meshing some of the teeth of the two carders together (but not scraping them past one another). *Lift* the right carder from the handle toward its front edge as you pull through and complete your rocking stroke—the engaged fibers from the left carder will lift from the teeth and surface of that card, and transfer to the right carder. Continue this rocking, lifting, brushing motion as you overlap the carders more and more. In the end, all the fibers from the left carder should have transferred to the right carder.

You need to go through the whole process once or twice more, or as many times as necessary to open and brush the fibers into a

To continue carding, transfer all the fibers back to the left carder by turning the right carder face up and holding the carders at right angles to each other. Start to lift the fiber ends extending from the front teeth of the right carder with the back teeth of the left carder.

The fibers will end up resting lightly on the left carder. Press them in place with your hand or with the back of the right carder.

60

completely uniform mass. To start again, *transfer* the fibers on the right carder back onto the left carder, as follows: Turn the right carder face up. Holding the carders perpendicular to one another, begin to lift the fiber ends extending from the front end of the right carder with the back teeth of the left carder. When the front end of the right carder meets the middle of the left carder, push the teeth of the carders together briefly so that the teeth of the left carder can get a better grip. Then you can continue to gently lift the fibers from the teeth of the right carder. All the fibers should now be resting lightly on top of the left hand carder (you might have a line of fibers down the middle that are more imbedded in the teeth). Now you just have to secure the fibers in the teeth of the left carder, which you can do by pressing them down with your hand, or with the back of the right carder.

Repeat the carding process as described until the fibers are straight and uniformly opened. Generally, two or three times through is sufficient.

To remove the wool from the right carder when you are finished, just lift it as you did before with the teeth of the left carder. You can then use the teeth of the right carder to lift any remaining wool from the left carder, to be sure all the fibers are free. This time though, there is no need to dig the teeth in for a better hold. You should now have a little batt of wool resting freely on top of the teeth of the right carder.

Place the right carder with the little wool batt in your lap so that the handle faces you. You'll notice that the bent teeth of the carding surface

The fibers on the top carder are ready to be made into a rolag. The line of fibers down the middle is normal. The fibers on the bottom carder need to be transferred and carded several more times.

To make the actual rolag, roll the little batt of wool toward the handle of the carder. Some spinners find it most comfortable to roll toward themselves and some like to roll away from themselves.

It's very satisfying to have a basket of rolags ready to spin. Once you have the idea of carding, you will find room for a lot of creativity in this process. The rolags below resulted from a color-blending experiment.

When you are ready to spin, join the fibers from one end of a rolag to your leader and begin.

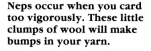

Neps occur when you card too vigorously. These little clumps of wool will make bumps in your yarn.

Loops can occur when the wool is placed incorrectly on the carders.

angle towards you, too. You can use that to advantage in forming the rolag. Starting with the fiber tips farthest from you, start rolling the wool jellyroll fashion toward you. As you roll with your fingers, keep the ends of the roll from expanding by controlling them with the heels of your hands. When you have the cigar shape completely rolled, pick it up, place it at the end of the carder farthest from you again, and once more roll it down toward you with just a bit of pressure. This will help compact the rolag and seal the free edge of the roll so it holds its rounded shape.

You can make a basketful of rolags at your leisure, and then sit down to spin. Pick one up, join the fibers from one end to your leader, and begin spinning. When you near the end of one rolag, pick up another, make a good join with the first, and continue.

Once you have the basic carding process down, you will begin to see all sorts of possibilities for blending colors on the carders. You can thinly layer the colors on top of one another, or place them side by side. Card thoroughly for a uniform blend and a heathered effect in your yarn. Blend them less completely for a stippled effect in your yarn. Or make a basketful of colored rolags that you pick up randomly and spin for a variegated effect in your yarn.

Problems in Carding

1) If you are too vigorous in your carding, especially when using the finer wools, you will find that you are making a lot of little tangled knots in the wool that are impossible to get out. These are called **neps** (or sometimes, **noils**), and are bits of broken and damaged fibers that tangle and cling together. Avoid making neps by carding more gently, being especially careful to avoid intermeshing the card teeth and raking them past one another. Card gently, as you would brush a small child's hair.

Another way that neps are formed is by starting a new carding stroke before the first one is completely finished. Be sure that there are no fibers still connecting the two carders at the end of a stroke before you return for another, or what you will be doing is folding the fibers over on top of themselves, and inviting tangles to form.

Neps are a common problem in home carding, cottage industry carding, and industrial carding, so don't feel bad if you see some in your wool, too. In fact, some spinners rather like the texture that they add to the batt or rolag, and thus the yarn. Just be aware that you will definitely end up with a textured yarn and not a smooth one—that is the nature of the beast. And neps, because they rest on the outside of the yarn, can make your sweater or hat look like it has already started pilling (pilling is the formation of small tenacious tangles of fibers on the surfaces of fabrics—a phenomenon caused by friction and wear).

2) If you let the fiber ends extend beyond the teeth at the handle end of the carder, they will tend to wrap around those teeth as carding progresses, leaving a visible line of looped fibers when the bat is transferred to the other carder. These lines of looped fibers are difficult to card out, frustrating your efforts to make a uniformly open batt of

wool. The more times you make looped lines of fibers, the more frustrated your efforts will be as you become more aggressive in your carding efforts in order to break them up. Take care to keep the fibers straight, and always well in front of the teeth near the handle.

3) If you put too much wool on your carder, it will take you much longer to do the job, it will be much less thorough, and you are likely to end up with neps as you work harder to control the unruly strands. Go through a trial run with two or three times as much wool as before, and see for yourself the poorer results.

4) The teeth on your carders may feel quite stiff in the beginning when they are new. Ideally, you want some ''give'' in the teeth, meaning that they will move back and forth a bit in their **card clothing** (the backing that the teeth are attached to). Teeth that are inflexible do more damage to the wool fibers. With use, the teeth on your cards will become more flexible, but it's a good idea to test their flexibility before you buy. They should move about a quarter inch when you flex them back and forth with your thumb. For wool cards, look for teeth about the size of a straight pin or finer, set about an eighth inch apart.

If you try to card too much wool at one time, it is more difficult to do a thorough job.

Combing

More spinners today prepare their wool by carding than by combing, even though in history combing is the far older process. Combing is enjoying a well-deserved comeback now and spinners have several sources from which they can easily acquire combs.

Wool combs aren't cheap, and the skill of using them is generally considered appropriate to the intermediate, rather than the beginning, spinner, so a full treatment of combing will have to wait for the next book. However, a basic understanding of the principles of combing will give you a comprehensive understanding of spinning methods.

Combing, like carding, opens and straightens the fibers in anticipation of the spinning process. But combing has the additional advantage of separating out the short and weak fibers from the long and strong fibers. At the end of the combing process, you have two products instead of one: **noils** or **milkings,** the short and tangled fibers, and a combed **top,** the parallel arrangement of the long and strong fibers. The noils are saved to card together with other noils or with other woolen preparations for woolen yarns; the top is used to spin worsted yarn. Worsted yarn is stronger, smoother, more lustrous, and more distinct in the fabric structure than the same yarn prepared and spun woolen. Hand woolcombing opens up a whole new side of wool preparation to handspinners.

Wool combs are much more formidable looking than carders are, as you can see. They can have anywhere between one and eight rows of teeth (referred to as the ''pitch'' of the combs) though more commonly, three to five rows are used. Carefully cleaned wool is **loaded (donned** or **lashed)** onto the first row or two of teeth of the stationary comb. The moveable comb, held in both hands, is then used to comb gradually from the tips to the base of the fibers, much as you would comb long tangled hair. The wool gradually transfers to the moving comb, and then back again to the stationary comb, as the work progresses. Once the wool is completely opened and all the noils are caught back in the tines of the combs, the long fibers are **drawn off** into a top through the eye of a **diz,** leaving the noils behind. With practice, hand combing can produce prepared fibers more efficiently than hand carding.

Semi-worsted Preparations

Although combs are unique in their effectiveness, there are other small tools that you can use to separate the shorter fibers from the longer ones while opening and straightening the fibers. Again, you'll need to start with clean locks of wool. Clamp a sturdy dog comb to a table edge. Grasping a lock firmly in the middle, draw the tip ends through the dog comb. Continue working back through the lock until you reach the middle. Reverse the lock in your hands, and repeat. Set the combed lock aside and do another.

When you have a stack of combed locks ready to go you can spin them with a worsted technique as well. The differences are that this is a less efficient way to remove short and weak fibers, and that you will have to make many more joins in your yarn (potential weak spots) since you won't be working with a continuous top.

You can also send away to England for **wool hackles,** which will do the same thing for you. They have longer teeth than dog combs and usually have two rows.

Wool combs produce a very even preparation. After combing has been completed, the wool is drawn off the combs through the eye of a bone or plastic tool called a *diz.*

While a dog *comb* **can substitute for wool hackles, a dog** *brush* **can pinch-hit for a flicker if you want to try this method of fiber preparation. Protect your knee with a piece of canvas or leather.**

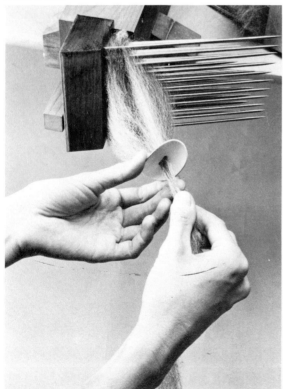

Flicking

Another fiber preparation technique is called **flicking,** and employs a small tool much like a miniature wool carder. Spinners use this method to prepare both greasy wool and clean wool.

Have some canvas or a piece of leather that you can use to protect your leg. Take a lock of wool and lay it across your knee. Holding it very firmly at the shorn end, tap the flicker through the tips of the lock and pull up and back in a quick motion. The movements are primarily up and down rather than back and forth. Work your way up to the shorn end, reverse the lock, and flick the shorn end as well. This method lifts and separates the fibers as they are being brushed and seems to be a bit easier on the fiber than the following method.

Instead of tapping up and down with the flicker, begin at the tip ends and just brush through the fibers. Work your way up the lock, reverse it, and flick/brush the shorn end. This method may be a bit more effective in removing dry, weathered tips from the wool, but you may well end up with more broken fibers in the teeth of the flicker than you would with the other method. Try both and see what you think.

If you pull too hard or place your hands too far apart when you condition sliver, it will become thin in places.

Conditioning a Commercial Sliver or Roving

Mill-produced slivers and rovings can become very compact by the time they reach you, through packaging, shipping, repackaging, and just plain old age. There is a quick way to recondition them with the loft

Recondition commercially processed sliver or roving by holding it with your hands about six inches apart and gently snapping.

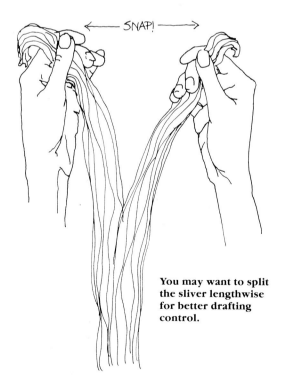

You may want to split the sliver lengthwise for better drafting control.

that will make drafting much easier and more pleasurable. This works for commercially combed tops as well.

Grasp the sliver at one end, with your hands about six inches apart. Gently snap the sliver four or five times until you feel the fibers just start to "give" or slip past one another. You don't want to thin or pull apart the sliver at all, you just want to get the fibers to barely start slipping past one another. Move your hands down one or two inches (no more) and repeat. As you go you'll notice the sliver starting to loft and soften. You need do only as much sliver as you plan to spin for that session, since the sliver you don't spin can still be stored compactly, and reconditioned as needed.

Slivers and tops are usually spun from the end, but when spinning very fine yarns from commercially combed top, some spinners prefer to split the top lengthwise for better control during drafting. First break off a three-foot length of top like this: Grasp the top on either side of the three-foot mark, with your hands six to eight inches apart. Gently pull the fibers until they completely slip apart. If the fibers won't budge, you are holding your hands too closely together. Take the strip of top and hold it up to the light looking for a naturally thin section running top to bottom. Separate the top there with a snapping motion, rather than pulling both sides gradually apart. In this way, you will minimize the disruption of fibers along the lengthwise break. Any time you do this, there will be some disruption of fibers, so take care to minimize that when you can. Split the section of top as many as three times, and spin each section from the end.

Exercises to Try

One of the best things you can do at this point is to take wool from the same source and prepare it by carding, combing, and flicking, so that you can see the differences in each. Take a small handful of clean wool and card it, ending up with a rolag. Take the same kind of wool and use a dog comb to straighten the long fibers and remove the short and weak ones. Then take the same kind of wool again and try flick carding it (you can use one end of your wool carder if you don't have a flicker). Make yourself a supply of each kind of preparation, for you will next want to spin them up and see how they behave in the yarn formation. Use the spinning techniques you already know and compare the results.

Then make yourself another supply so that you can practice the drafting and spinning methods coming up next.

Your choice of fiber preparation techniques affects your yarn profoundly, whether it is made from white fibers or hand-dyed locks like the ones in this picture. There's a small amount of a green-based dyelot at the upper left. The more brightly colored fibers at the center top have been prepared and spun in four different ways, producing yarns which have different color effects and textures.

At the lower left is a rolag. The yarn spun from it is even and the color is lively—almost iridescent— but relatively uniform.

In the center is a lock which was flicked with a dog brush. The resulting yarn is smooth and lustrous, and retains some of the color variations, particularly those from the tips of the locks.

At the right are two yarns—one small skein and the large skein—which were spun from very lightly teased locks of wool. These are the most heavily textured yarns and preserve the dyelot's color variations most vividly. The thicker yarn appears to be the most brightly colored because the color changes occur most frequently.

The miniature niddy noddy is handy for making sample skeins.

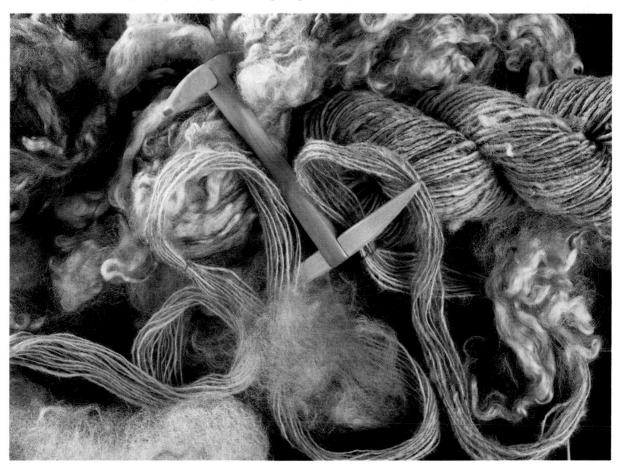

This shawl is both lightweight and warm. Spinning—from a "rainbow batt" of blended colors—was a constantly changing pleasure. Although woven in twill on a four-harness loom, it could also be made in plain weave on a rigid heddle loom with a 10-dent heddle.

A Lightweight PLUM SHAWL

Designed by Deborah Robson

The yarn for this lightweight shawl was spun from a "rainbow batt", which was made by feeding different colors of wool into a small industrial carding machine. The colors—predominantly fuchsia and plum—were partially blended in the process.

This size yarn

YARN: Approximately 1200 yards of handspun singles, at 2000 yards per pound. Layers were peeled off the batt and then separated lengthwise into strips, which were spun in sequence for a gradual change from one shade to the next. Care was taken to prevent weak spots in the yarn, and only one warp end needed to be repaired during weaving. The spinning sequence of the skeins was maintained and was followed in warping and weaving.
SETT: 10 ends per inch.

WARP LENGTH: 3⅝ yards.
WIDTH IN REED: 20 inches.
TOTAL WARP ENDS: 200.
DRAFT: A twill was chosen, for its draping qualities and in order to pull each color to the surface for 2-thread floats. Any simple twill can be used. The pattern was not obvious in the finished shawl.
TAKE-UP AND SHRINKAGE: 15% in width and 10% in length.
WEAVING: The first and last picks of the shawl were woven in plain weave, to give an even base against which to work the twisted fringe. A straight 2/2 treadling sequence was followed for the full weavable length of the warp.
FINISHING: Four warp ends were included in each grouping for the twisted fringe. A knot was tied in each twisted group 7 inches from the edge of the weaving. The shawl was washed in warm water and dishwashing liquid, spun in a salad spinner, and laid flat on towels to air dry. It was lightly steam-pressed when dry.

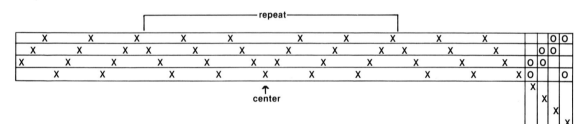

The actual repeat is the area included in brackets. It's easiest to thread in a balanced way if you start at the center and thread toward the sides. With this particular twill, the two sides balanced with a total of 199, rather than 200, warp ends.

Natural-dyed yarn samples were used to decorate the yoke on this sweater. You could use small amounts of color-blending experiments or dyed roving. The sweater's size and gauge can be adjusted to fit both the yarn and the intended wearer.

A RAINBOW SWEATER
Designed by D. Lorraine Chilton

Like the hat on pages 36-37, this sweater begins with a sample swatch. It can be made to fit anybody. Again, you adjust the pattern to your yarn—a great trick when you want to work with handspun! Many of the principles in this way of thinking about knitting have been "unvented" (her word, meaning discovered or re-discovered, as universal truths are) by Elizabeth Zimmermann. If you want to know more about her method, look into *Knitting Without Tears* (Charles Scribner's Sons) or one of her other books.

You can work the sweater in a single color, or you can use color-and-texture bands, as shown. If you experiment with color-blending in carding or with natural dyeing, your samples can find an appropriate home in a design like this. When you work colors into the yoke, the body can be any neutral shade.

This size yarn

YARN: Between 1 and 1½ pounds of handspun singles, made from white Romney wool spun directly from the fleece. Some individual Romney sheep have wool that is a little too coarse for a sweater of this type; this wool is both sturdy and soft enough to be comfortable. The exact amount of yarn depends on the size and length of the sweater. Set the twist and block the yarn.

NEEDLES: Knit on two circular needles (16-inch and 32-inch), in a fairly large size as compared to those you would use for commercial yarn of the same grist, so the texture will show and the yarn's softness will be retained in the finished project. This sweater was knitted on size 8 needles. You may also want to use a set of double-pointed needles at the beginning of the sleeves.

GAUGE: Cast on approximately 25 stitches and knit until the sample is 5 inches long. Determine the gauge as described on page 36.

The body of this sweater is worked first, up to the underarms. It is worked in the round. The sleeves are also worked on circular needles to the underarm. Then the three pieces are joined. The yoke is worked in one piece on a large circular needle, and if you are using colors you can add them as you go.

Determine the number of inches you want your sweater circumference to be (usually the chest measurement plus between 2 and 6 inches of ease, depending on how loosely you want the sweater to fit). Multiply the circumference by the gauge. Remember this base number, because you will refer to it several times.

Body: Multiply your base number by 90%, or .9. Cast on that many stitches, using the large circular needle. Work in K1, P1 ribbing for about 2½ inches (join the first and last stitches at the end of the first round, making sure no stitches are twisted and placing a marker between these stitches). Add 10% more stitches by increasing one in every tenth stitch around the sweater. The total number of stitches will now equal your base number. Change to stockinette stitch and work until your sweater is the length you want it to be at the underarm point.

Sleeves: Multiply your base number by 25% or .25. Cast on that many stitches, using the small circular needle or double-pointed needles. Work in K1, P1 ribbing

for about 2½ inches (join as for body and work in the round). Change to stockinette stitch. Knit plain for 4 rows. On the next row, increase 1 stitch on each side of the marker (2 stitches in all). It will look nice if you increase into the second stitch from the marker, instead of the stitch right next to it. Repeat this increase every fourth row until you have a number of stitches equal to 33% of your base number, or your base number times .33. Work straight until your sleeve is the length you want it to be to the underarm. Make the second sleeve in the same way.

Yoke: Next you will put the three pieces of the sweater together on the large circular needle. In the process, you need to reserve stitches at each underarm point. These will later be woven together to form the underarm.

Place a second marker on the sweater body (a safety pin will do) to divide the total number of stitches in half. Multiply your base number by 8%, or .08. At each sleeve marker and at each of the two body markers, reserve this number of stitches (half on each side of the marker), using a stitch holder or a piece of scrap yarn. Don't bind the stitches off.

Begin to knit the yoke. Work half the body stitches, then one sleeve, the other half of the body stitches, and the second sleeve. Place a marker before you begin the second round. In the first few rounds of the yoke you may find it awkward to have all these pieces on one needle. Bear with the difficulty, which will disappear soon.

Knit for about 1 inch before you start the first color ring. Start the color at the marker (the section following it will be the back of the sweater). Knit one row of accent color and then purl two rows of that color. Return to the main color and knit one row. Continue with this pattern, add-

ing colors of your choice until the yoke is half completed. How do you know when that is? The total length of the yoke from underarm to neck will be 25% of the sweater body circumference *in inches*, so when the yoke is half completed it will measure half that number.

Begin to shape by decreasing. In a white row, K1, K2 together throughout the round. Continue with your color pattern until the yoke is three-quarters finished. Work another decrease round. Continue to work straight again. Work a final decrease round when the yoke is completed and you will have the correct number of stitches for your neck.

Neck shaping: The back of the neck will fit better if it is slightly higher than the front, so you need an additional six rows on the back half of your sweater.

Mark the back stitches by placing a string or safety-pin marker at the midpoint of each shoulder. Starting at the left-hand shoulder, purl across the back. Turn work, slip the first stitch, and knit across the back, knitting two additional stitches at the end of the row. (Do not increase stitches; just knit existing stitches held for the front of the sweater.) As you knit the first of these two stitches, it is helpful to pick up a thread from the stitch below and knit it with the first of these two stitches. This does not add a stitch; it does reduce the chance that a hole will be visible when you turn. Continue alternating these purl and knit rows, slipping the first stitch in each row, until you have an additional 12 stitches on your needle (6 rows).

Neck: Continue around the front so that you are again knitting a circle. When you reach the beginning of the round, work in K1, P1 ribbing for 1 inch. Bind off loosely.

Finishing: Join the underarm seams by weaving them invisibly.

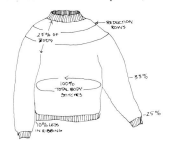

Drafting and Spinning Techniques

How you control the drafting and twisting of fibers is the second vital ingredient in yarn construction. The amount of control you can exercise at this stage depends upon how thoroughly you have prepared your fibers: smooth, open, clean preparations allow you to make smooth yarns, while preparations with neps, short fibers, or dirty fibers will result in textured yarns, no matter what you do. As a result, fiber preparation and spinning technique go hand in hand.

Take a moment to analyze a prepared fiber form before you begin to spin. This will help you decide what kinds of yarns it might be suited for. Grasp a number of fiber ends and pull them out from the supply. How long are the fibers? Are they randomly arranged or smoothly aligned? Are there neps? How stiff or flexible are the fibers? How clean? Do they have a very fine diameter? Are the fibers uniform in thickness and length, or are some fine, downy fibers mixed in with longer, hairier ones? Are the fibers straight and slippery, or crimped (wavy) and elastic? When you rub a bit of fiber on the sensitive skin of your neck and face, is it soft and silky, or harsh and scratchy? The answers to these questions hold clues about the kind of yarn you will want to spin from this fiber.

The other factor affecting the yarn you will produce is the spinning technique you will choose. A number of possibilities are described below.

If you had a perfect fiber preparation and were able to completely control the drafting and twisting processes, each time you drafted out a bit the same number of fibers would be separated from the fiber supply, they would always be drawn out to the same length at the same rate, and they would always be twisted to the same degree. Taking this ultimate control a step further, the motions of drafting and twisting would never be separated. Instead, the fibers would flow continuously and smoothly into the yarns as they were being twisted. In order to control yarn formation to the greatest possible extent, work at refining your skill so you will have this uniform and fluid set of motions available when you need it.

On the other hand, you want to learn to use design techniques at will to make a wide range of different yarn styles. By learning different drafting methods, you can make the most of yarn design possibilities. Part of the intrigue of handspun yarns is that they can be made better, and in more varieties, than the yarns found in stores. Handspun yarns are unique creations, with the fiber content, color, size, ply, texture, and performance completely in the hands of the spinner.

The terms *woolen* and *worsted* are sometimes used to describe spinning techniques as well as fiber preparations. When applied to spinning, they refer to the tendency of the yarn to turn out fuzzy and full (woolen) or slick and compact (worsted), as a direct result of the method used to spin the fiber. An example of a woolen technique would be the inchworm; the best example of a worsted technique is, of course, the worsted technique itself. You might also see the terms *semi-woolen* and *semi-worsted.* Spinning from the fold can be called a semi-worsted technique because the controlled flow of fibers results in a comparatively smooth yarn. The same can be said of the long draw. On the other hand, the double draw tends to result in yarn with a fuzzy surface, and thus is labeled woolen or semi-woolen.

Woolen-type and *worsted-type* are descriptions more often applied to yarns than techniques. They usually refer to a yarn prepared through a combination of fiber preparation and spinning techniques that do not necessarily match, like a carded preparation spun worsted. Depending on its final appearance (more fuzzy or more slick), the resulting yarn may then be described as woolen- or worsted-type.

You'll see these terms used interchangeably in many publications, so don't be thrown by them. In most cases, what name to use for a process or a yarn is a judgment call.

One-handed Techniques

You have already learned a one-handed draw—the one you used when spinning on the supported spindle. You had only the drafting hand to control the flow of fibers; the other hand was kept busy controlling the spindle, and thus the amount of twist that entered your yarn.

One-handed spinning usually implies that you pull the fiber supply away from the wheel as the yarn forms (rather than the yarn being pulled into the wheel from the stationary fiber supply). You spin out a length of yarn, then allow it to wind onto the bobbin. You will soon see that the better the fiber preparation, the easier the job is for the drafting hand.

The long draw, which is the spinning technique you used on the supported spindle, is easily adapted to the flyer wheel. This is essentially the same method which has been used for centuries past on hand spindles, great wheels and charkhas. It is called the long draw.

Set your wheel for medium take-up tension. Start your draft from six to eight inches in front of the orifice. Use your drafting hand to move in a gentle arc from orifice to arm's length as you let the fibers play out just ahead of the advancing twist. Keep the other hand six to eight inches in front of the orifice, and use it as a twist monitor: pinch and let go quickly when you need just a moment of extra tug to draft against, otherwise let that hand just hover over the yarn. Keep your eye on the drafting zone, and play out the fibers so that the drafting triangle stays the same shape: long and narrow for lower twist yarns, and short and wide for higher twist yarns. When you reach the end of your draw, let the yarn quickly wind on until there are only six or eight inches left in front of the orifice. Begin your long draw again and continue spinning.

With a well-prepared fiber supply you can make a remarkably controlled and even yarn with this method. You have to be a bit brave in your drafting, moving faster than you're used to. But the best yarn is made by a smooth continuous sweep of the drafting hand. The long draw works very well with any fiber preparation that drafts smoothly and evenly, whether it contains neps or not. Use the long draw with slivers, rolags and carded batts.

The long draw has several advantages over other drafting methods. It can be speeded up significantly as you gain confidence and experience, especially when your fiber preparation is smooth and even. It allows you to see the yarn over a distance, so that you can monitor any changes in texture or size. And if you see a slub or thin area in your yarn that needs to be corrected, you have time to stop the wheel and deal with the problem before the yarn disappears into the orifice.

Spinners with back trouble or aching shoulders sometimes choose to shorten the length of the long draw, so that the torso and shoulders don't have to twist quite so much. The general principle for this medium draw is the same as for the long draw, though.

Spinning from the fold is another way to use the long draw to advantage. When you are starting with combed top but find it difficult

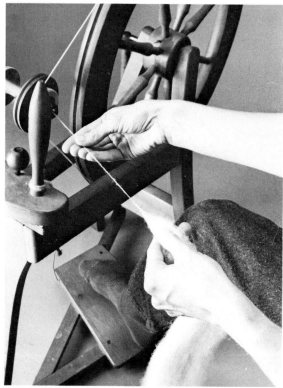

In the LONG DRAW, the drafting hand moves away from the wheel in a gentle arc. The fibers feed out just in advance of the twist.

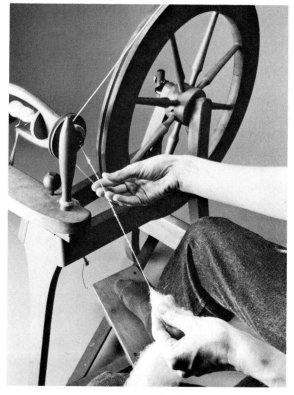

The right hand stays about six inches in front of the orifice and hovers over the yarn, as shown. You can use it to pinch and let go quickly when you need a moment of extra tug to draft against.

to spin from the end, you can change to this technique. Pull off a piece of top about as long as the fiber-length. Take the piece of top (it shouldn't be any more than six inches long) and fold it in half across the first knuckle of the forefinger of your drafting hand. Look to be sure that the ends hanging down from your fingers are exactly the same length, and then tuck them into the palm of your hand with your remaining fingers.

Pull out a few fibers from the folded section of the top that is closest to your fingernail. Make your join there, and begin to spin. The fibers will be folded in half as they flow into the yarn over the point of your finger. Let the fibers feed so that the folded top is used up gradually from your fingernail to your knuckle.

Keeping the ends of the top even and tucked away in your palm is important so that you draft from the center of the fibers and not from one end. If you don't keep the fibers neatly feeding from the center fold, you will end up with a tangle in your palms.

Spinners are often tempted to use a section of top which is longer than a single fiber-length. On trying this, they find that the middle third of the fibers feeds off as it should, but the ends don't. Two-thirds of the long piece becomes disordered and unmanageable.

Some spinners find that controlling the flow of fibers for this kind of spinning is easier if they hold the fibers across their curled fingers and parallel with their thumb. Spin from the center of the fiber by letting the fibers feed from between the first and second fingers.

This is a fast and smooth way to spin combed top using the long

Fold a short piece of top in half across the first knuckle of the forefinger of your drafting hand.

To spin FROM THE FOLD, pull out a few fibers from the folded section of the top that is closest to your fingernail. Join and begin to spin. Keep your finger pointing toward the orifice.

The fibers will flow off the end of your finger smoothly. Hold the fibers with their ends tucked away. You can use your second hand for occasional assistance.

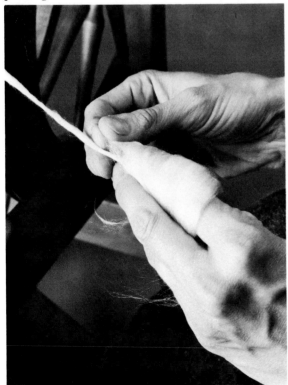

draw. The disadvantages are that the yarn will be a bit weaker because the fibers within the yarn are now half of their original length and many more joins have been made.

Two-handed Techniques

Two-handed drafting methods rely on a tugging pressure between the hands to regulate the size and texture of the yarn, rather than using the pull of the wheel.

The **push-pull** or **inchworm technique** that we spoke of back on page 46 is a two-handed draw. It is very similar to the drafting method you used when you were practicing with the drop spindle.

Hold the fiber supply stationary. With the hand closest to the wheel, pull some fibers an inch or two out of the supply and toward the wheel. Let go of the drafted segment and let the twist enter it. At the same time that you draft the fibers toward the wheel, a little length of yarn disappears into the orifice (you "pull" from the fiber supply and "push" into the wheel). Your drafting movements should be small and quickly repeated, with all the motions staying directly in front of you. The twist will enter the short, drafted lengths quickly and intermittently.

You'll make a smoother and more even yarn if you pull on the just-spun yarn itself, right where the twist meets the drafted fibers. If, instead, your fingers reach into the drafting triangle to pull more fibers,

In the INCHWORM technique, your fiber supply hand stays in one place. The hand closest to the wheel pulls some fibers forward.

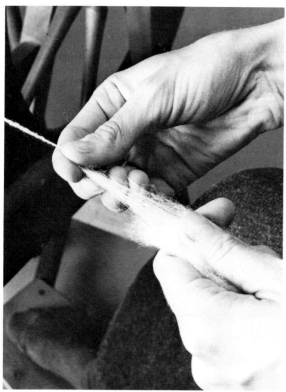

Then the hand closest to the wheel moves back and gets ready to pull out the next group of fibers.

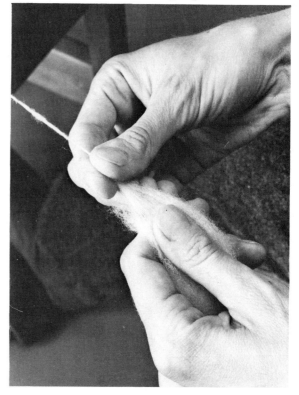

a slub will result at each pinched place. You can certainly use this as a design element in making a thick and thin yarn by regulating the size and the spacing of the slubs—just vary when and how far you reach into the triangle.

The inchworm method cannot be speeded up as much as the long draw. It does allow more minute control over the texture of the yarn if the spinner is skilled. Many beginning spinners start out with the inchworm method because they feel it gives them more control—they feel more secure if they can control the yarn at *both* ends and move slowly.

The **double draw** is a method where drafting happens *twice*. The first time, the yarn is drafted quickly to an intermediate length of thinned roving with a minimum amount of twist—just enough to hold the fibers together. Then that length is drafted again between two hands as more twist is allowed to enter, until the yarn reaches its final length.

Hold the yarn with the hand nearest the orifice while you draft rapidly back until you have about a two-foot length of elongated sliver or roving. As you draft, the hand near the orifice should quickly open and close around the yarn to let in just a little twist in order to hold the roving together. You'll see that the twist jumps to the thin places in the roving and skips over the thicker slubs—that's just what should happen. Now pinch the roving with your fiber-supply hand so that no

In the DOUBLE DRAW, your front hand will control the twist more decisively than it did for the long draw. Pinch off the twist while the drafting hand moves quickly back, elongating the roving. Release the front hand just often enough to let in a little twist.

Then pinch with the *drafting* hand, so no new fibers are drafted. Continue to let in twist intermittently with your front hand. Gently pull and elongate the roving between your hands. The yarn will even out. When you are satisfied, let it feed onto the wheel.

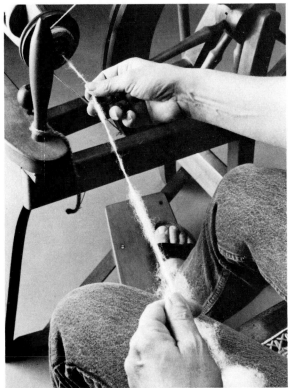
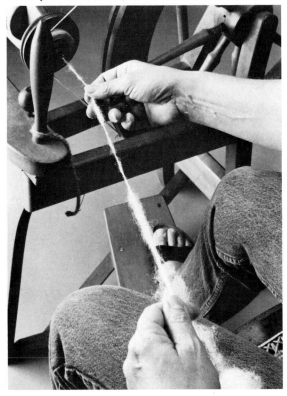

new fibers will be drafted. Pull and elongate the roving between your hands as you let more twist in intermittently as needed. You should see the slubs drifting apart and shrinking to the size of the thin areas of your yarn. Continue pulling between your hands and letting in twist until the yarn appears even in size and twist amount.

This method takes a little practice because it is all too easy to let in too much twist during the first draft, making the second draft difficult or impossible. It is also hard to make an even yarn, because the slubs rarely slip apart to just the size you want them to—they either stay too big or they suddenly pull apart to a size that is too thin. And one more caution: this technique tends to make a fuzzier yarn than other methods.

The **true worsted draw** slicks all the fiber ends down just as the twist enters that portion of the drafted fibers. That is what makes a worsted yarn so smooth and lustrous.

Set your wheel for a slightly stronger take-up than you might use for normal drafting. Make your join and begin spinning with combed top. Pinch the twist off with the hand near the orifice. With the fiber-supply hand, draft back two or three inches—about half the fiber-length. *Without* releasing the pressure of the pinching fingers, slide those fingers up the drafted length so that the twist follows immediately behind them. The fibers are compacted and held together as your fingers slide over them, so the twist catches them in that position before

In the WORSTED DRAW, your front hand will maintain its pinching pressure at all times. Draft back half a fiber-length with the fiber supply hand.

Then slide the front hand back, so the twist enters the newly drafted fibers. Continue to draft and slide, making sure that no twist appears *between* your hands at any time.

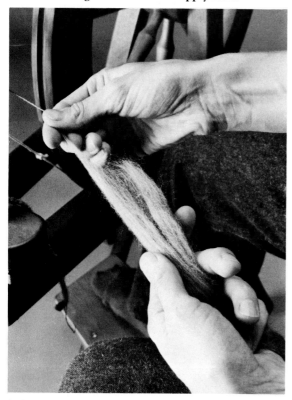

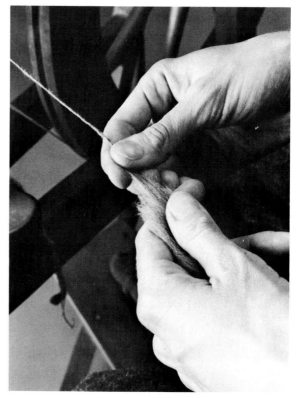

they are released. Thus all the fiber ends are caught in the twist instead of springing loose to form a "halo" along the yarn length. Draft another half-fiber-length, and slide your fingers along as the twist follows behind.

Take care that twist is never allowed in the space between your two hands. Try to draft the same amount of fiber each time so that your yarn will be even. If you draft more than half a fiber-length each time, your yarn will gradually get thinner and thinner, because the drafted fibers won't be enmeshed enough with the fibers in the supply to pull the next ones out. You can draft a length shorter than half a fiber-length, but your hands will have to work faster to make the same amount of yarn.

Take extra care to keep your fiber supply loose, open and neat. You can help that by resisting the temptation to clamp down on the fibers with your thumb. Keep your hand open, thumb up, with the combed top just lying across your four fingers. If you need just a little extra resistance to draft against, you can very gently hold the fibers with your last two fingers.

Worsted spinning can be speeded up quite a bit with practice. You can use the worsted draft as a sort of modified push-pull technique by working right in front of yourself, winding on each short length as you draft the next (the fiber supply stays stationary). Or you can try it as a modified long draw by winding on an arm's length after you have spun it out to your side (fiber supply moves away from the wheel). Try both and see which is more comfortable.

Some Notes on Spinning Commercially Prepared Fibers

When you are breaking off a length of sliver or top to spin, be sure that your hands are farther apart than a fiber length so that you're not tugging on both ends of the same fibers. The sliver or top should slip apart easily—if it doesn't, move your hands farther apart and try again.

Commercial (mill-made) slivers usually draft more smoothly from one end than from the other, so if the flow of fibers seems particularly jerky no matter what you do, flip the sliver over and try drafting from the other end.

If the sliver is thick, you may have trouble getting the fibers to feed evenly from across the open end instead of feeding from somewhere down the side of the sliver. All you need to do is turn your wrist so that the twist begins to catch the fibers from the end again, and continue spinning.

Combed top can be spun from the end using the long draw, but most often results in a yarn with regularly spaced slubs about a fiber-length long. For now, try spinning combed top with the worsted technique, or from the fold. Later on, with patience and practice, you can learn to produce an even yarn by spinning top from the end with the long draw.

Plying

Plying is the process of respinning two or more yarns together into a larger yarn. One of the most common plied yarns for spinners is a two-ply yarn: two single yarns, both spun with a Z twist, are put back through the wheel and spun together, this time with an S twist. Plying both strengthens the yarn and evens out size and twist irregularities. Two-ply yarn is especially popular for knitting and crocheting, and for warp yarn in weaving.

By plying the singles in the opposite direction from their original twist, two desirable things occur. First, the Z-twist and the S-twist energies tend to neutralize one another. If it's done just right, the result is a stable or **balanced** yarn, i.e., one without excess twist energy, that does not try to untwist itself. Second, since the single yarns are partially untwisting as they are plied, the two-ply yarn looks and feels softer than the original singles.

Plying on Your Wheel

First, be sure there's an *empty* bobbin on your flyer. Have two bobbins of Z-twist yarn ready to go. These bobbins will need to be able to rotate freely. If you have a lazy kate with your wheel, mount the bobbins on that. You can also slip them onto knitting needles that are resting in holes or notches cut in a shoe box. Or you can ply from balls if you wish, made by hand or with the help of a ball winder. Put each ball in a wide-mouth jar or bowl so it can unwind freely without rolling across the floor.

There are lots of simple devices which will keep your bobbins or balls of yarn from wandering while you ply.

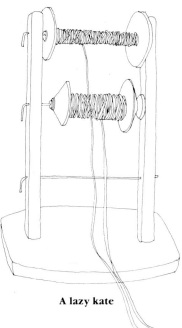

A lazy kate

A shoebox and two knitting needles

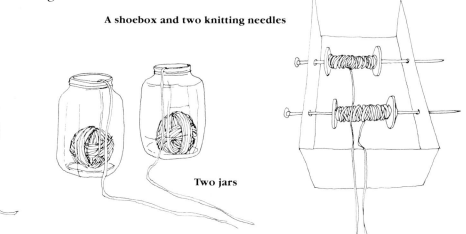

Two jars

Put the bobbins or balls of yarn to one side and just in back of you—line things up so that the single yarns can feed off the bobbins or balls freely, pass through your hands, and be wound directly onto the wheel. Adjust the take-up tension on your wheel to give you a little stronger pull than you used to spin your singles. You'll need less twist in the ply than you did for the singles (about two-thirds as much). You want the yarn to be able to pass through your hands more quickly, and the wheel to take it up readily.

Take one yarn end from each bobbin or ball, plus the leader, thread these three strands as one, and tie a slip knot. Your leader must be a two-ply itself, or a singles spun in the S direction, or you will unspin your leader when you begin. An alternative is to thread the two ends of your singles through the orifice and over the hooks, and tie them directly to the bobbin. Hold your two singles taut in one hand, with a finger separating them. Start the wheel rotating *counterclockwise,* or in the S direction.

The hand farther from the wheel will hold the yarns *evenly taut* and the strands separate. The hand closer to the wheel will control the movement of the twist.

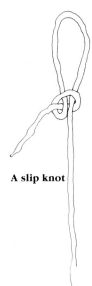

A slip knot

To *ply* S-twist

The most basic type of plying takes two Z-twist singles and combines them with an S-twist. Done just right, this produces a balanced yarn which is softer and loftier than the original singles. A simple test, explained on page 84, will let you know as you work whether your plied yarn is balanced.

To *spin* Z-twist singles

There are two preferred methods for you to try. In the first, the hand closer to the wheel also holds the yarns separate with a finger. With an arm's length of yarn held taut and stationary by your rear hand, slide the front hand along the yarn from a point near the orifice (about six inches away) outward to the other hand, at a pace just ahead of the advancing twist. This action helps to "lay" the yarns down in the ply with a minimum of abrasion and fuzzing. When your hands meet, pinch off the twist with your moving hand (hold the yarn tightly so the twist can't move any farther along the yarn), and feed the plied yarn quickly into the wheel. At the same time, release tension slightly on your rear hand so that the next length to be plied is pulled through those fingers, even and taut, ready for plying. The sequence is slide, pinch, feed; slide, pinch, feed. The twist is never allowed into the yarn held between your two hands.

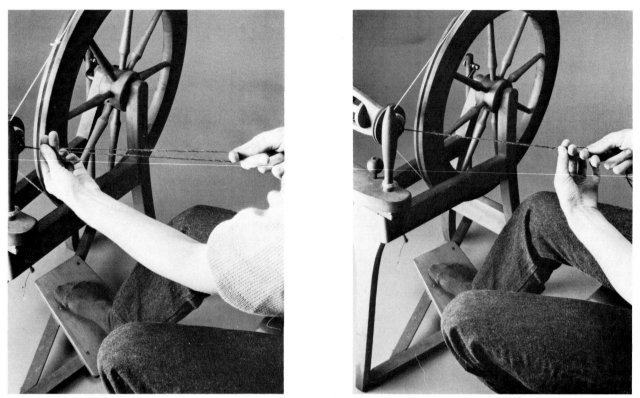

In the first plying method, the front hand moves while the rear hand stays still. The front hand slides back ahead of the twist. When it reaches the back hand, it pinches off the twist and moves forward again to let the yarn feed onto the bobbin.

In the second plying method, the front hand remains in one place while the rear hand moves. The front hand pinches off the twist. The back hand moves back, preparing the separate strands to become yarn. Then the front hand releases the twist, which races toward the back hand. The back hand keeps it from going further and feeds the yarn onto the wheel.

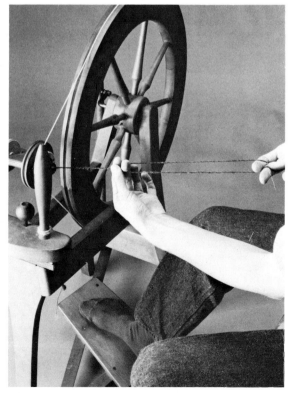

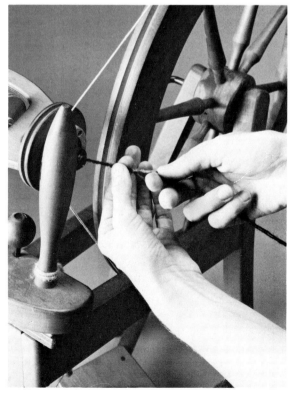

In the other method, it's the rear hand that does the moving. Start off with both hands near the wheel this time. Pinch off the twist near the orifice with your front hand, while you slide your rear hand back for another length of taut yarn. Then let your front fingers go completely, so that the twist races up the yarn to your rear hand. The rear hand keeps the twist pinched off at that point so it will not travel any farther. When there is sufficient twist in that length, quickly feed in the plied length until your two hands meet. Your front hand pinches off the twist again, and the process continues. In this case, there is some slight abrasion as the yarns rub past one another as they twist. Lumpy yarns will not be plied as evenly with this method—just as in the original spinning, the twist will tend to jump to the thinner places in the ply and skip over the slubs. Plan for that if that is a design element you want in your thick-and-thin yarn. Just keep in mind that your two-ply will be more abrasion-resistant (and therefore less susceptible to pilling and wear) if the slubs are wrapped with the other yarn.

As a third alternative, you can try holding a single yarn in each hand while letting the wheel pull them from you steadily as they twist together. You will be holding the two arms of an upside down "Y"—the stem of the "Y" is where the singles meet and twist together. The two singles must be held at the same tension (difficult, with two different hands doing the regulating). Check your tension constantly by looking at the formation of your "Y"—the stem should stay exactly midway between the two arms, and the arms should always be the same length. The take-up tension on your wheel will have to be adjusted carefully so that the wheel pulls the yarn from you at just the right pace for the twist you want. As you can tell, this method is difficult to control well.

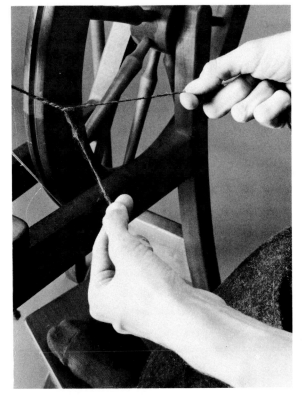

A third plying method, which is harder to control, places one strand of yarn in each hand. The yarns are plied and fed onto the wheel at the same time. The take-up tension has to be adjusted precisely and each hand needs to hold its strand of yarn with exactly the right amount of tension.

In any of these methods, holding each yarn under the same tension is necessary for an even ply. If one yarn is held too tightly, the other will wrap loosely around it, and that results in a very different look and feel. As an experiment, hold the yarns as in method three, and try varying the amount of tension with which you hold each yarn—one taut and one loose. Watch what happens to the structure of the plied yarn. For an even ply, aim to have the two yarns wrap around a common (though invisible) axis, rather than one yarn wrapping around the other.

How much twist do you want in the ply? If you want a balanced yarn, you want just enough twist in the ply to cancel the twist in the singles. There is a simple test that you can perform periodically along the length of the yarn to see how well you're doing. Hold a two-foot plied length of yarn between your hands. Bring your hands together, and watch what happens to the slack loop of yarn. If it doesn't twist on itself—good work!—you have a balanced yarn. If the loop twists in the S direction, you have put too much twist in the ply. If it twists in the Z direction, then there is not enough twist in the ply. Keep checking your yarn as you go and adjusting the amount of twist in the ply as necessary.

Just how tight a ply you can make in a balanced yarn will depend on how much twist you put in your singles. Although a yarn may be balanced, it could also have too little twist in the singles, and then in the ply, to make an attractive or easily knitted yarn (knitting needles often get caught between the strands of a loosely plied yarn). On the other hand, you can get a very tightly plied yarn from starting with two tightly spun singles, but then your yarn will not be particularly lofty or

Top left: **Both strands of yarn evenly tensioned.** *Top right:* **The white strand was held under greater tension than the other strand, which wraps around it. The tension on the looser strand varied from time to time.** *Bottom left:* **Seriously overtwisted in plying!** *Bottom right:* **Undertwisted in plying. The strands wrap around each other, but are only loosely joined.**

Check for balanced plying by stopping for a moment and reserving an arm's length of plied yarn before it feeds onto the wheel. Move your hand forward so the yarn hangs in a loop. If it makes a graceful curve like this, your plying is balanced. This test works best with freshly spun yarn. If the singles have been sitting on the bobbin for a while, do a test with a similar, new batch of yarn and then ply the "older" yarn so it looks the same.

soft. Take a look at other yarns you like, and then experiment with different twist amounts in your singles and plies to get a yarn that looks good and performs well for you.

Unbalanced yarns have their place, too, for special effects in fabrics. Here the spinner must be careful in setting the twist (see Yarn Finishing).

Plying on Your Spindle

Here are two methods to try on your drop spindle. The first is similar to the one the Peruvians use. When you have two spindles full of Z-spun singles, hold them relatively close to one another, but stationary, so that the yarns can be unwound simultaneously. The Peruvians hold the bottom of the spindle shafts with the toes of each foot and unwind the yarns from the tip of the shaft. You can also rest the spindles on their sides in grooves in a box so that the yarns unwind from the sides of the shafts as the spindles turn. Wind the two ends together into a ball, treating the two ends as if they were one (try to maintain an equal tension on each yarn).

Put the two-strand ball into a bowl and attach the free end to your spindle. Spiral the yarn up the shaft (remember to turn your spindle *counterclockwise* this time, in the S direction) and secure it under the hook or make a half hitch as necessary. Ply the two yarns together in the S direction (some spinners like to switch the spindle to the other hand for S twisting—use whichever hand feels more natural). Wind on as before, in the same direction as used for plying.

In the other method you start with two balls of singles. Put each in a bowl or basket to control its movement as it unwinds. Once you attach the yarns to the spindle, use the same method as above, being sure to keep the two yarns under equal tension as you go.

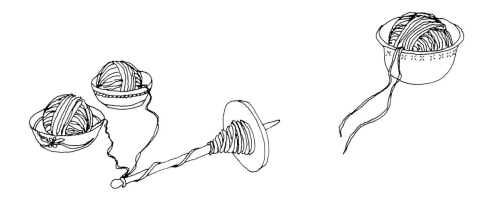

More on Balanced Yarns

Balanced yarns need little further processing, and, of course, work very well in a multitude of woven, knitted and crocheted projects. A plied yarn need not be exactly balanced to perform well, since **yarn finishing** (processes like washing and drying under certain conditions) will **set** the twist (stabilize it, making it permanent for all practical

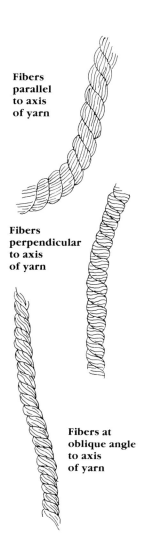

Fibers parallel to axis of yarn

Fibers perpendicular to axis of yarn

Fibers at oblique angle to axis of yarn

purposes), and make the yarn quite tame. Just aim for a naturally balanced yarn, checking it as you go, and it will work very well.

Balanced yarns are superb for knitting. Properly spun and finished, they can be softer and much more elastic, and have more body than similar yarns from knitting shops. Handspinners find that a balanced yarn is the best to use for knitting in plain stockinette stitch—otherwise there is a danger of the fabric slanting, and no amount of blocking later on can make up for it. Many knitters prefer a balanced three-ply yarn for its softness, loft, extra body and drapability.

Analyzing a Plied Yarn

Here's a quick trick that will tell you at a glance if a spun yarn is essentially balanced, or at the least, if it has been spun in one direction and plied in another. Take a look at the illustration. Focus first on the individual fibers in the yarns. What direction are they running? If they are parallel to the axis of the yarn (straight up and down) then the yarn can be considered balanced. To find out what direction of twist the spinner used, look at the direction of the ply. If it is S, then the singles were spun Z, and if it is Z then the singles were spun S.

If the fibers run perpendicular to the axis of the yarn (side to side), then the yarn was not made to be balanced, but rather had plying twist added in the same direction as the original spinning twist. Again, you can check the direction of the final ply to see what twist direction the spinner was working with.

If the fibers lie at an angle to the axis of the yarn, neither perpendicular nor parallel, it's a good idea to untwist the yarn at some point, and take note of what the unplied singles look like. You can do this at the end of the yarn, but you'll get a more accurate picture if you do it somewhere along the yarn's length where untwisting ends don't interfere with your analysis. This last technique can be used on just about any type of yarn construction you run into, no matter how fancy and complicated the plying sequence used.

Special Effects with Plying

Plying offers you an unlimited vista of design possibilities. You can make three-, four-, and even eight-ply yarns out of various combinations of naturally colored or dyed singles. They can all be Z-twist, of the same size and twist amounts, plied S; or you can start combining various yarn types in any manner that pleases you. Not only can you combine colored yarns, yarns of different sizes, and yarns with different twist directions and amounts, but you can ply together yarns of different fibers, like silk and wool, or Angora rabbit and camel down. Experimentation is the game and the school.

Any single that is plied in the same direction at its original twist will have twist added to it, rather than subtracted from it. It will be more compact, and more lively with twist energy. As a design technique, spinners can combine, say, one Z single and one S single, and ply them S. The Z single will lose some twist and grow puffier and softer in the process. The S single will gain twist, and become harder and smaller.

The effect that you get is a yarn that looks much like a string of beads: a "bead" yarn.

"Cabled" yarns can be made with a sequence of plying steps. Two Z singles are plied S. Two of the S-plied yarns are then plied Z. This makes a very interesting and durable yarn, particularly effective when two colors are used.

Plying does take more time, not only in the plying phase itself, but in spinning all the singles necessary for the final yarn. But the design possibilities are limitless, and your product is a unique yarn that will last and last.

Special effects in plying can become challenging and rewarding. Shown are (1) a single yarn, (2) a two-ply, (3) a bead yarn with one dark ply and one light ply, (4) a cabled yarn made from a dark two-ply and a light two-ply, and (5) a cabled yarn made in one color.

Yarn Finishing

One of the most important factors contributing to a yarn's behavior and appearance is **finishing.** This refers to the processes you put the yarn through before you weave or knit it up into fabric. Finishing steps can include washing, rinsing, dyeing, steaming, weighting, blocking, and setting the twist. The whole idea is to get the yarn to its finished state *before* it goes into your garment, rug, or placemat—you don't want any surprises later when your piece is first wetted or washed.

The most important of the finishing steps is setting the twist: giving the fibers in the yarn a "memory" of their new position, so that they stay there, and do not try to untwist. Setting the twist in a yarn can be done in a variety of ways, depending upon the fiber and how permanent the set needs to be, based on the final product and the procedures used to make it.

Wool and Other Animal Fibers

Merely leaving yarn on the bobbin for a few days imparts a temporary set, often making it easier to handle in other processes like plying or skeining. A more permanent set results from thoroughly wetting the skein in water and letting it dry. The hotter the water, the more permanent the set (although you don't want to go above about 200° F on wool yarn, or fiber damage may result).

Washing your skeins in hot water with mild detergent, and rinsing them in hot water, not only cleans the yarn but gives it a moderately permanent set. Use the washing and drying methods described on page 32 ("Processing Your First Yarn"). Be gentle; soak the yarn clean rather than wringing and twisting it, to avoid felting the strands together.

The most permanent set is given by steaming the yarn. Steaming the wool fibers for two minutes or longer will actually break old chemical bonds and form new ones, changing their internal structure to conform to their new shape. To steam your yarn, you can hold a taut skein over a steaming tea kettle for several minutes. Use a niddy noddy or two sticks to hold the skein while you steam it. Be very careful to keep your hands and arms out of the way—steam burns happen in an instant and are quite painful. The skein can be left on the niddy noddy or laid upon a towel to dry.

Another, and safer, steaming method requires a hand-held steamer from a fabric or small-appliance store. Wind the yarn on a reel or niddy noddy, and gradually go around the skein with the steamer so every part is thoroughly steamed. Then leave it on the reel or niddy noddy to dry.

Blocking refers to wetting the yarn and letting it dry to shape. Knitters most often wash or wet their skeins and let them dry in a relaxed state on a towel. This encourages yarn loft and elasticity. Weavers more often wind their yarn off from bobbin to reel and steam them in place, letting them dry under tension, or wash them and hang them with a weight to dry (see page 33). This results in a less elastic, more stable yarn that will be easier to warp and weave with. The fabric will be finished again when it comes off the loom, and at that point the yarns will be encouraged to relax.

Wool is often dyed after it's spun into yarn. The dyeing procedures, which include wetting and heating, will also set the twist.

Silk

Silk can be finished by wetting the skein in warm water and letting it dry on a towel. This works well for woolen-spun silk yarns. Silk can be wound on a reel or niddy noddy and moistened with a cool water spray and left to dry, or it can be steam set. These last two methods help preserve the smooth, lustrous appearance of your silk if it was spun from combed top. Smooth silk yarns may feel stiff when dry, but all you have to do is work them gently with your hands to restore the softness.

The extra step that you might have to take in finishing silk yarns is degumming. Most silk fibers available to handspinners are already degummed, but you may run across a partially degummed fiber. Put your skeins in a generous amount of soapy water (use a mild dishwashing liquid). Gently bring the skeins to a simmer and hold there for about thirty minutes. Follow with a rinse of about the same temperature, using clear water to which a bit of vinegar has been added. The yarn should feel soft and drape well once it is dry and you've worked it a bit. If it is stiff, there is still some sericin remaining on the fibers, and you may need to repeat the procedure.

Cotton and Linen

Cotton and linen yarns can also be temporarily set by leaving them on the bobbin for several days, but this method does not work nearly as well for these fibers as it does for wool. For a more permanent set, boiling the skeins is more effective. These fibers can take much higher processing temperatures than wool and other animal fibers; boiling will not harm them.

Both cotton and linen have a waxy outer coating (consisting of cellulose, fats, waxes, and pectic materials) which makes water penetration difficult. Boiling skeins of these yarns helps water reach the interior of the fiber (pure cellulose), where the heat and moisture do their job of setting the twist. Boil the yarn in skeins or wind it onto pieces of PVC (plastic) pipe that have holes drilled in them. (Winding the yarn on the PVC pipe will help you control it if it has a lot of curl and twist.) Skeins of cotton yarn will float at first, but sink as the boiling water penetrates their waxy coating. *text continues on page 94*

Fun and toasty LOOPY MITTENS

Designed by Phyllis Rodgers

Phyllis Rodgers submitted these ingenious mittens to a contest run by *Spin·Off* magazine to locate the "World's Warmest Mittens." They were among the winners—and she had made them from her very first handspun yarn. The palm is flat stockinette, and the back is a loop stitch.

This size yarn

YARN: Two-ply handspun about the size of knitting worsted, about 4 ounces. Phyllis used Romney wool, which rates well for both durability and reasonable softness.

GAUGE: 4½-5 stitches to the inch.

NEEDLES: Size 6 (American), single-point.

Cast on 30 stitches.

Cuff: K 6 rows in garter stitch (K every row). (This will give you 3 ridges.) Work in K2, P2 ribbing for 9 rows.

Main part of mitten: You will work one pattern for the palm, on the first 15 stitches in the row. You will work the loop stitch for the back of the hand on the second 15 stitches in the row. Place *two* stitch markers at the midpoint of the row; you will later increase stitches for the thumb between these markers.

For palm:

Row 1 (right side): K1, sl 1, for 15 stitches.

Row 2: P15.

Loop stitch pattern, for back of hand:

Row 1 (right side): K across.

Row 2: K1; to make a loop in the next stitch, * insert needle in next stitch as if to knit, wrap yarn around right-hand needle once and around 2 fingers of left hand and right needle twice, then complete the K stitch (there are now 3 loops on the right-hand needle), K1, repeat from * across.

Row 3: K1, * K3 loops together, K1, repeat from * across.

Row 4: K across.

Repeat rows 1 through 4 for pattern.

Work palm and back of hand simultaneously for enough rows to fit hand from wrist to beginning of thumb.

Continue patterns for palm and back of hand *at the same time* that you increase 2 stitches for the thumb on each *right side* row, between the markers. Repeat until there are 12 stitches between the markers. Place these 12 stitches on a stitch holder.

Continue in patterns on 30 stitches for 6 more rows, or until the mitten is long enough to reach the top of your little finger.

Begin to decrease. Continuing patterns on palm and back of hand, K2 together at the beginning of every other row for 6 rows (24 stitches remain). P 1 row. K2 together across row (6 stitches remain).

Break the yarn, leaving 12-18 inches of tail. Thread the tail through the final 6 stitches, tighten, and secure with a small stitch. Do not cut the yarn; after completing the thumb, you will use it to sew the seam down the outside edge of the mitten.

Thumb: Place the 12 thumb stitches on a needle. K1 row, P1 row, and repeat for 6 rows, or until the thumb section is as long as the thumb. Decrease as for the mitten, with a row of K2 together. Break the yarn, leaving a 6-inch tail. Thread this through the remaining 3 stitches and then sew the thumb seam.

For the SECOND MITTEN, you will reverse the instructions by working the *loop pattern* on the first 15 stitches in each right-side row and the *palm pattern* on the second 15 stitches in each right-side row.

What if *your* first handspun yarn helped you win a prize? These mittens were judged to be among the warmest anywhere.

The Perfect WINTER WEEKEND SWEATER

Designed by Marilyn Livingston

Although patterns which develop from the gauge of your yarn are a neat way to knit with handspun, you can use your yarn with commercial patterns. Gauge becomes more important than you ever believed it could be—make your swatch large enough, and pay attention to half- and quarter-stitches in your results. Change needle sizes until you get the gauge you want. Then you will have no limits.

This pattern was adapted for handspun yarn from a Bernat pattern (as long as your gauge matches that of the pattern, you need not make specific "adaptations" because you are using handspun). Directions are for a small (size 8-10) sweater, with changes for medium (12-14) and large (16-18) in parentheses.

This size yarn

YARN: 1250 yards of two-ply handspun at approximately 660 yards per pound (about 2 pounds of wool). This was spun from a color-blended commercial roving.
GAUGE: In stockinette on size 9 needles: 7 stitches = 2 inches, 5 rows = 1 inch.
NEEDLES: One pair each of sizes 6, 9, and 10, or the sizes you need to obtain the correct gauge.

Back: Using smaller needles, cast on 56 (66, 74) stitches. Work K1, P1 ribbing for 1½ inches. Knit the next row, increasing 9 stitches evenly across the row—65 (75, 83) stitches. Change to size 9 needles. Starting with a purl row, work even in reverse stockinette (purl right-side rows, knit wrong-side rows) until piece measures 13½ (14, 14½) inches, or desired length to underarm. Put a marker on each side of work to mark start of armholes. Continue to work even in reverse stockinette until piece measures 5½ (6½, 7) inches above markers, ending with a purl row.

Yoke: Knit the next row, increasing 12 (14, 14) stitches evenly across the row— 77 (89, 97) stitches. Change to size 10 needles and work in K1, P1 ribbing as follows: *Row 1:* K1, * P1, K1, repeat from * across row. *Row 2:* P1, * K1, P1, repeat from * across row. Repeat these two rows until work measures 8 (9, 9½) inches from marker, ending with row 2.

Shoulders: At the beginning of each of the next 2 rows, bind off 20 (25, 28) stitches.

Neck facing: Continue to work in ribbing as established, increasing 1 stitch on each end of every row for 10 rows. Maintain the rib pattern. Facing should measure 2 inches. Bind off loosely in ribbing.

Front: Work to correspond to back until the piece measures 8½ (9½, 9¾) inches, ending with a K row. Work in pattern stitch (described below) until piece measures 13½ (14, 14½) inches. Mark each side for armhole. Continue to work in pattern until there are 52 (52, 56) rows of pattern—5½ (6½, 7) inches above markers.

Pattern stitch for front: Stitch is worked over 55 rows, creating a V shape, defined by a K1, P3 rib, widened every 2 inches with an increase worked on both edges of the V shape. This increase and the change in needle size help compensate for the drawing-in of the rib. *Row 1:* P 32 (37, 41), K1, P 32 (37, 41). *Rows 2-10:* Work stitches as established. *Row 11 (increase row):* Purl to the fifth stitch from the first K1, P increase in next stitch, K1, * P3, K1 *. Repeat from * to *, completing established pattern, P3, K1, P and inc 1 in next stitch, P remaining stitches. *All other rows:* Work stitches as established, or as they present themselves. Work an increase row every 2 inches: in *rows 21, 29, 37, 43, and 49* for all sizes, *and also in row 53* for the large size.

Front yoke: Change to size 10 needles and work K1, P1 ribbing as follows: *For small and large sizes:* K1, * P1, K1, repeat from * across row. *For medium size only:* Inc 1 stitch in first stitch, * K1, P1, repeat from * to last 2 stitches, K1, P and inc 1 stitch in last stitch. *For all sizes,* repeat the

following two rows until piece measures 8 (9, 9½) inches above markers, ending with row 2. *Row 1:* P1, * K1, P1, repeat from * across row. *Row 2 (right side):* K1, * P1, K1, repeat from * across row.

Shoulders and neck facing: Work front same as back.

Sleeves: Sew front to back at shoulder seams. With right side facing you and size 10 needles, pick up and knit 72 (82, 86) stitches along arm edge between markers. Work in K1, P1 ribbing for 2½ inches, ending with a right side row. Knit the next row, decreasing 16 (18, 20) stitches evenly across the row—56 (64, 66) stitches.

Change to size 9 needles and, starting with a P row, work in reverse stockinette, decreasing 1 stitch at each end every 1 inch 12 (12, 14) times, then every ¾ inch 0 (2, 0) times.

Work even on 32 (36, 38) stitches until piece measures 14 (15, 16½) inches, ending with a P row. Knit the next row, decreasing 8 stitches evenly spaced.

Change to size 6 needles and work in K1, P1 ribbing for 2½ inches. Bind off loosely in ribbing.

Finishing: Sew underarm and sleeve seams. Fold neck facing to wrong side and hem in place.

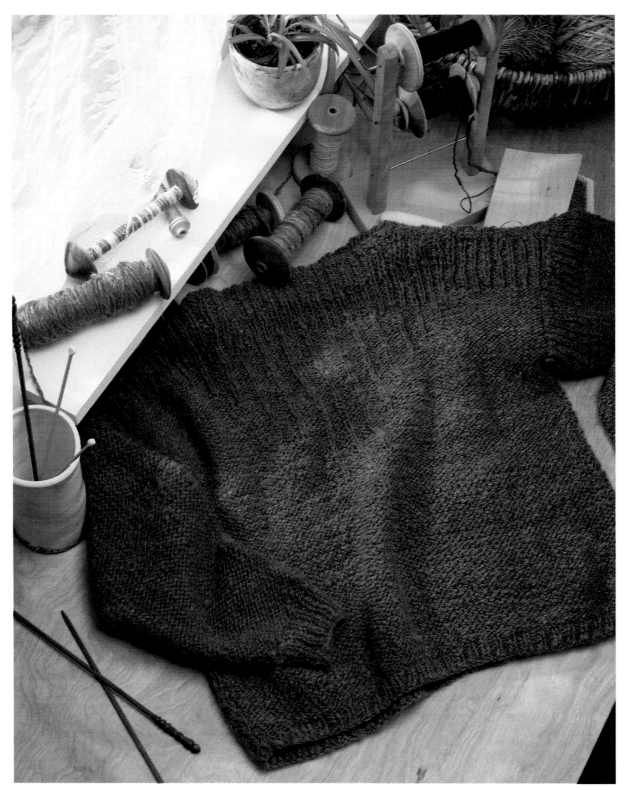

Worked in reverse stockinette with a diamond-shaped pattern on the yoke, this sweater knits up easily and will become a standby in your wardrobe.

After you've boiled cotton skeins, you will probably have tea-colored water left in the pot. This may cause a slight discoloration of the yarn. You can get cleaner skeins if you boil them first in soapy water and then in clear water. You can also use weak solutions of household bleach to whiten cotton.

Linen yarns are wiry and harsh when spun, but will soften and lighten in color if boiled, as above, in several baths of soapy water, followed by a clear water rinse. Dry linen under tension, using a reel, a niddy noddy, or weights. Linen, which is a grayish-tan in its natural state, can be whitened with a mild solution of household bleach, or by the older method of hanging the yarn in the sun and wetting and turning it at intervals.

Linen fabrics can last a lifetime, or longer. This fiber has the unique property of getting softer and more lustrous with wear and laundering —it is the one fiber that gets better with use.

Storing Your Wool and Yarn

It would be lovely if we could display all our handspun wool yarns in baskets around the house, for they're a pleasure to look at, and continually inspire us with project ideas. The danger, however, is that your precious handspun skeins, and your unspun wool, whether washed or unwashed, will become a feast for the two kinds of pests that are the spinner's bane.

Perhaps the more commonly known and identified pest is the wool moth, whose larvae dine on our fine woolens. There are two types of wool moth to watch out for: the casemaking clothes moth and the webbing clothes moth. The adults are tiny (one-quarter inch long) buff-colored moths that seem to dart rapidly and randomly around the room. They fly in from the outside, especially in the warmer months, and seek a nice warm, dark, still place to lay their eggs. An inch inside your yarn or pile of raw wool is perfect, as are your stored winter sweaters.

The eggs are white translucent spheres smaller than the head of a pin. The emerging worms are white with brown heads; they are quite small, perhaps one-sixteenth inch long in the beginning, but they quickly grow to one-half inch. It is at this growing stage that they do their damage. If there is plenty of food, they will be content to stay put for quite a while, munching away.

If you look carefully among your woolen treasures and see what looks like brown sand, that's a telltale sign that the worms are (or have been) there—it is their excreta. If you see a white case, a sort of finely woven cocoon one-quarter to three-eighths inch long and open at each end, that is another sure sign—and the little varmint is probably still inside. If you see a webbing of fine white silky filaments, beware the intruder. And one more sign—if you notice a fine rain of fiber fragments when you take your fibers out, you probably have been visited by these pests.

Wool moth larvae eat any animal fiber except silk. The larvae will feed voraciously on things like Angora rabbit hair, dog hair, raw or clean wool, camel down, cashmere, and even the tiny bits of skin that may cling to the fibers.

The other pest, which we don't hear about as often but which is just as destructive, is the carpet beetle. Like wool moth larvae, carpet beetle larvae feed on protein. They are often found under carpets and in the cracks and crevices in flooring. Carpet beetle larvae eat all the protein fibers—including silk.

The adults are roundish, hard-shelled beetles about one-eighth inch in diameter, and are a mottled brown color. They feed on flower pollen, so you must beware of letting them have a free ride indoors in your spring bouquets. The larvae are about the same size and shape as the adults, but they are soft and have hairy bristles. The larvae prefer dark, quiet, unventilated corners just like the wool moth larvae.

The best safeguards against moth damage (besides the poisons like mothballs, which I cannot bring myself to use and therefore cannot recommend) are careful storage and constant vigilance. When you buy new fibers, and especially when you receive free fibers, inspect them carefully before you bring them into the house. The larvae don't like light or moving air; if you go through your stored fibers and garments regularly, you can air them out and inspect for early warning signs. Even if you don't find any signs of infestation, it's a good idea to expose fibers to a bit of sun and breeze. Vacuum the room thoroughly before you repack your fibers.

If you *do* find signs of infestation, take the fibers outside immediately. If damage is extensive, drop the whole bag in the garbage without a backward glance. If damage is minor, you can try drowning the eggs and larvae by submerging the fibers for twelve hours or more, or you can freeze them at near 0° F for several days.

Store wool and other protein fibers in paper bags that are taped shut (the worms don't eat the cellulose of paper bags), and then put them in cardboard cartons. Label the bags and cartons with the contents, and put a small sample on the outside in a self-sealing plastic bag.

Plastic bags themselves often afford good short-term protection if wool moths or carpet beetles are not a big problem in your area (they seem to prefer lower altitudes and humid climates). But there are two things to be aware of: moth larvae eat through plastic bags when they're hungry enough, and clean but unspun wool tends to felt when stored in a tightly closed plastic bag. (The fibers become permanently entangled because of the movement of moisture and any changing temperatures.)

Fragrant herbs can also be successful in discouraging moth and carpet beetle infestation. Be sure and freshen the sachets often, and place them and your fibers in a tightly closed box or chest to contain the vapors.

Cellulose (plant) fibers, like cotton, flax, ramie, and hemp, are rarely attacked by insects. Silverfish, crickets, cockroaches, and termites may chew a few holes in these fabrics (especially if they are starched), but they find most of their food elsewhere. You do have to be concerned with mildew and funguses, though, so keep these fibers dry, and expose them to sunlight from time to time.

Selecting and Spinning Fibers

WOOL is the downy or hairy outer coat grown by sheep. Some older breeds of sheep grow both: a downy undercoat, and a long hairy outer coat. Most of the modern breeds now have a single coat. The length of the sheared fiber, called the **staple length,** can be from two to fifteen inches, depending on the breed; the diameter, luster, crimp, and color can vary just as much. Washed wool varies in color from a creamy white through tans and browns, and from silver through grays and black.

Crimp, the three-dimensional waviness along the length of the fiber, is a naturally occurring property of wool. Crimp adds a little extra friction between fibers, which helps in drafting. Finely crimped wool is associated with short stapled fleeces of fine diameter; when the crimp looks more like long open curls, it is associated with the long luster wools.

The wool fiber has an outer sheath of overlapping scales along its length. The scales on wool contribute tremendously to its propensity to **felt.** In conditions of heat, moisture, and agitation, wool fibers curl and interlock with one another until they cannot be pulled apart. Taken to the extreme, they shrink and mat into a dense, thick fabric. This felting property can result in disaster if fibers and yarns are washed too vigorously. But it can also be used to advantage in the **fulling** process after a fabric has been taken from the loom. The fabric, stiff and coarse when it comes off the loom, is washed and gently agitated until the yarns and fibers relax, fluff up, and intermesh to the desired degree.

Wool is available to the handspinner in a variety of forms, from raw fleeces to combed top. It can be carded into slivers, rovings, and batts, in natural or dyed colors. One popular preparation is the "rainbow batt", where multiple dyelots of wool have been partially blended.

Fine, short wools, like Merino, Rambouillet, and Cormo, are suitable for the softest garments to be worn next to the skin. Prepare them carefully to avoid neps, and spin them to a fine diameter.

Cross-bred and medium length wools, like Corriedale, Columbia, Polwarth, Finn, and Perendale, make excellent handspinning fleeces. These wools are used extensively for sweaters, hats, mittens, gloves, and jackets—almost all outer wear. Some of the finer and first clip fleeces (the first fleece sheared from a year-old animal is called a *hoggett* fleece) can often be used for next-to-the-skin wear as well. These are good fleeces for the beginner.

Crimp can be fine, as in the bottom lock, or coarse, as in the top lock.

The outer layer of a wool fiber is a sheath of overlapping scales.

Shortwool and down breeds, like Suffolk, Hampshire, Dorset, and Jacob, have been used by handspinners for centuries. They are sometimes described as "spongy" in texture, and they lack the softness and sheen of the other short wools, but are suitable for outerwear garments.

Longwool and luster breeds, including Romney, Border Leicester, Lincoln, Coopworth, and Cotswold, are much prized for their use in worsted yarns. Their length and glossy surfaces contribute to strong, lustrous yarns that can be knitted or woven for outer garments. These fibers can also be prepared and spun woolen, and some of their sheen will still show through. The fibers of the longwool breeds resemble mohair.

Coarsewool and mountain breeds include Scottish Blackface, Cheviot, Black Welsh Mountain, Karakul and Rough Fell. The fleeces are used for hardwearing fabrics and carpets.

Some people have an adverse reaction to wool, but it is good to remember two things. One, wool is made of the very same substances that our own hair and fingernails are made of. Two, most of the wool on the market feels harsh—it has been commercially processed (and none too gently), and probably has many additives on the fibers—mothproofing agents, permanent press treatments, and even resinous coatings—that can cause allergic reactions. Give your allergic friend a hat or scarf made of fine, soft, hand-processed and handspun wool, and see if that makes the difference.

SILK is produced by the larvae of several moths, but white culti-vated silk comes from the *Bombyx mori.* There are several other types of moths that produce usable silk. The best known group produces **tussah** silk, produced in shades of light to dark honey-tan. The silk from these worms is coarser than that from the *Bombyx mori.*

Both tussah and bombyx silk are available to handspinners as combed top, **bricks** (combed top that has been folded into a compact block), carded slivers and batts (usually found in various grades that include neps; often called silk noil), cocoons (both raw and degummed), and **mawata** or **caps** (cocoons that have been opened and stretched over a frame producing thin sheets of silk fiber). Occasionally the spinner may find several kinds of **silk waste** available; these are shorter fibers left from industrial processing.

To spin combed top or bricks, use the procedure described for wool top. Spinning from the end will be difficult, and even worsted spinning will take some practice. To start out, spin silk top from the fold, either over the finger or from the palm. You will get a very glossy, smooth yarn.

Carded slivers and batts can be spun as is. Spin from the end of a sliver; take handfuls or strips from the batts to spin. Carded silk gives a textured, matte-finished yarn.

Degummed cocoons, mawata, and caps can be spun as is. If you have a cocoon, tweak one end until you loosen some fibers from the mass and begin to spin. With a mawata or cap, you may want to see if you can separate its layers—often a number of cocoons have been stretched and formed on top of one another. If you have a square mawata, just start spinning from one corner. If you have a bell-shaped cap, start spinning from the point of the cap. Silk in all these forms can be fluffed up or turned into roving, processes which aren't difficult but also aren't necessary for you to discover the pleasures of silk.

Silk waste may need to be degummed (see page 89) before spinning, and will probably need carding. Spin as for carded batts and slivers.

A wonderful, luxurious fiber, silk can be used in an unending array of woven and knitted products. Scarves, sweaters, gloves, shirts and blouses, baby booties—all these next-to-the-skin garments made with finely spun and plied yarns are suited for the combed silks and carded silk blends (for instance, mixtures with fine Merino wool or Angora rabbit hair). Rougher silks work very well in skirts, jackets, outer sweaters, shawls, and even towels and washcloths.

COTTON is the fluffy seed coating found in the pods of plants of the genus *Gossypium*. Cotton is picked by hand or by machine. It is then ginned to separate the fiber from the seed and to remove dirt and plant material. The longest, silkiest, finest cotton fibers are the Sea Island and Pima (American-Egyptian) varieties. These are available to handspinners, though most of the cotton available in the United States is of the shorter American Upland variety.

Cotton comes to handspinners in the forms of combed top, carded sliver, and just ginned. Since cotton fibers are so fine and short, they need to be spun into a very fine yarn in order to hold together. The yarn diameter needs to be small enough so that each fiber can wrap around the yarn several times—the diameter of a paperclip wire is just about right. (If you need a bulkier yarn for a project, ply several single strands together.)

Set your wheel for minimum take-up tension, and move your drive cord to the smallest flyer or bobbin whorl you have to increase the amount of twist entering the yarn with each treadling. The drafting triangle will be tiny. Cotton can be spun very well on supported spindles and charkhas; start there to get a feel for drafting and twisting a fine yarn without take-up tension, and then move to your wheel. Remember to test occasionally for adequate twist.

Combed top is difficult to spin from the fold because the fibers are so short. Try spinning top from the end instead, using the long draw. Carded slivers spin easily from the end with the long draw. Inchworm spinning doesn't work well with cotton, again because the fibers are so short, and the drafting zone is almost invisible. Some spinners like to use double drafting—give it a try.

If you have ginned cotton, you'll probably want to tease it first, or card it on cotton carders, to open the fibers before you spin. If there is vegetable matter in your ginned cotton, some may fall out with carding, but you'll have to pick out most of it by hand.

When spun evenly and smoothly, cotton can be used as warp; it works especially well when it is plied. Weft yarns can be spun as singles or can be plied, and here the evenness of the yarn is not nearly so critical. Plied cottons in a variety of textures work very well in knitting—the structure of knitted fabrics adds the elasticity that the fiber itself lacks. Tightly spun singles and plies can be used for crochet work, like lacy edgings for towels. Because of its breathability, coolness, softness, and easy laundering, it can be used in a variety of situations, from those calling for next-to-the-skin comfort, to filet lace curtains, to jacket fabric, to rug warp.

FLAX is a **bast** fiber—taken from the inner stalk of the plant. Once spun, flax is called **linen.** Flax is available to handspinners as **line** or **tow.** Line flax is usually sold in **hanks,** softly twisted groups of fibers that look something like a skein. Tow usually comes in combed top form with fibers about six inches long.

Spinning line flax is both picturesque and enjoyable (this is where a spinner's **distaff** comes in, to hold the prepared fibers), but it is beyond the scope of this book. Begin your study of linen with tow in the form of combed top.

Spin tow from the fold, using your forefinger. Spin it wet, if you wish, with either saliva or water kept on the fingers of the right hand only, for a smoother yarn, or dry for a hairier yarn. Try spinning it worsted from the end as well, either wet or dry.

Tow linen is suitable for weft use, but don't try using it for warp unless it is spun very evenly and tightly plied. If spun fairly fine and plied, tow linen can be knitted into a lacy summer sweater. Linen fabrics get softer and more lustrous with use.

MOHAIR is a long lustrous fiber produced by the Angora goat. Younger animals give much finer, silkier, curlier hair than older ones, so kid mohair is in demand by the handspinner.

Mohair is available as raw fleece (scour, and card or comb, as you would for wool), carded sliver, carded batts (often dyed in a rainbow of colors), and combed top. Look before you buy; some raw mohair is heavily matted (pass it by), and some commercially carded or combed mohair lacks luster and body. Set your wheel for light to moderate tension (the fibers are slippery), and choose your whorl size based on the diameter of yarn that you want. Spin as you would for wool.

Mohair weaves well into coat, jacket, and upholstery fabrics. It takes dyes very well, adding a silky shine. Mohair does not have the loft that wool does, so knitted and woven fabrics made purely of mohair, especially in worsted, will be heavy and compact. Many handspinners like to blend mohair with wool of a similar length to take advantage of the luster of mohair and the loft and softness of wool.

CAMEL DOWN is the soft undercoat of the camel, naturally shed each year. The longer, hairier outer coat is quite coarse.

Camel down's natural color is tan to reddish-brown. It is sold as an open mass of fibers, in sliver, or in top. The best camel down is very soft, uniform, and free of guard hairs. It is a luxury fiber that will feel like something between fine wool and cashmere.

Set your wheel for light take-up tension, and move the drive cord to the smallest flyer or bobbin whorl to get the most twist per treadle—the set-up you need for fine yarns. Spin the open mass as is, tease it if it has condensed, or card it lightly on cotton carders. Spin sliver from the end; spin top either from the end or from the fold. Make a fine yarn with medium twist. Set the twist as you would for wool.

Camel down is suited for all types of next-to-the-skin garments and even outerwear. Ply it for knitted garments of all kinds, or weave with it for everything from light scarves to jackets.

CASHMERE, the undercoat that is combed from the Kashmir goat, is one of the finest, softest fibers available. Fabrics of cashmere are deliciously soft, warm and comfortable.

There are several colors and a range of qualities available to the handspinner; the supply seems to continually change, however. Look for bags of fiber that are free from guard hair, and that contain fiber that is not matted or tangled. Epidermal scurf (dry skin flakes) is common to see in the fiber, but since it is very difficult to remove, the less you see, the better.

You can spin the cashmere without any further preparation—it comes in a loose mass. Tease it a bit or card it if you want to (use cotton carders, because they are much gentler on the fiber). Adjust your wheel for a light take-up tension, spin fine, and aim for a moderate rather than a light twist. Because the individual fibers can vary quite a bit in their length, from less than an inch up to three inches, you'll feel the fibers trying to draft at different rates—little puffs of short fibers will try and slip quickly by with the longer fibers. That calls for a bit more control with your drafting hand. This time you'll want to closely control the passage of fibers into the drafting zone by pinching them between your finger and thumb. Your drafting triangle will be quite small.

For knitting, make a two- or three-ply balanced yarn for scarves, hats, gloves, or luxury sweaters. Cashmere can also be used for weaving —just be sure any warp yarns you use are smooth and strong. Try blending cashmere with silk at the fiber stage, the plying stage, or the fabric stage, for unique and elegant garments.

LLAMA and **ALPACA** belong to the camel family, but are native to the South American Andes.

The llama is larger, and is the South American beast of burden. It can now be found on farms in the United States as well. The llama has two coats—a soft, wooly undercoat and a straight, hairy outer coat, though breeding practices have tended to meld the two. The fibers come in lovely natural shades of white and brown.

Alpacas produce a fleece with finer and stronger fibers than llamas. The finer fibers need to be separated from any guard hairs. The natural colors of the fibers are white, browns, and black.

Llama and alpaca are sometimes available as raw fleeces, but more often as combed top. The alpaca top that you buy should be very silky and soft; the fibers will have little or no crimp. The llama will be slightly coarser. Spin the top from the fold, using a moderate tension on your wheel. Both these fibers make a very dense yarn, so sweaters may tend to sag, and weavings may seem heavy compared to wool. Blends at the fabric stage can work very well, if you keep in mind that wool will relax and take up during the fulling process and the alpaca or llama fibers will not. For knitting, try blending these fibers with wool before you spin.

ANGORA RABBIT hair is a very fine and silky fiber. Handspinners prefer that the hair be plucked rather than shorn, because it is longer and has no blunt end, and therefore seems to shed less.

Buy fibers that are long (about four inches) and without matts (tangled clumps of very fine fibers). No washing is necessary. Some spinners like to just tease the fibers before spinning; others prefer to card the fibers on cotton carders. This is another fiber that you will want to spin very fine with low tension on your wheel. Spin from the teased mass or from the end of the carded rolag. If the fibers are very neat, you may be able to fold locks of the hair over your forefinger and spin it from the fold. Don't make an effort to spin a fuzzy yarn because the fibers will fluff out from the yarn as it is worked in knitting or weaving. And if you spin a fine, smooth yarn now, the fibers will shed less in the final piece.

Angora blends very well with silks and fine wools at the fiber stage, the plying stage, or the fabric stage. It is extremely soft, and so is used for next-to-the-skin garments.

QIVIUT is a rare fiber—the downy undercoat of the musk ox, which makes its home in the far north. Qiviut has been spun by the Inuit peoples for years, and is gradually becoming more available to handspinners in general.

The fiber may come with bits of grasses and seeds mixed in, and will almost certainly have to be separated from the guard hairs mixed in with the down. After handpicking it clean, prepare and spin this fiber as you would cashmere.

The End and the Beginning

This book just opens the door into the world of natural fibers and the yarns that can be made from them. There are many paths you can follow from here to expand your knowledge and give you inspiration, but beware: you may begin to lament your lack of time to pursue them all. A friend once described spinning as "the continuous thread." And it's true—the thread gradually disappears into the distant past, but extends an unknown distance into the future as well.

We have just touched on fiber blending and unique yarn constructions. The whole world of natural and synthetic dyes awaits you. Learning about and using twist energy in ways that only a handspinner can will introduce unique fabric structures unavailable by any other means.

What about growing your own flax and learning how to process it from seed to finely woven linens? You can grow and process your own cotton, too. Or learn about sisal, henequen, ramie, milkweed, abaca, banana, hemp, pineapple, and numerous other fibers. Want to raise your own fiber-bearing animals? Angora rabbits make good pets and fiber producers for spinners whether they live in the city or the country. And then there's raising your own sheep or Angora goats or even llamas.

There is quite a fascinating history behind spinning, not only in the western countries but all over the world. All kinds of tools and techniques introduced over the centuries can be rewarding to investigate and reproduce. You may want to search out, and perhaps even collect, some of the many amazing styles of spinning wheels used over the years. You may want to try making some of your own modern tools, like spindles, distaffs, spinning bowls, lazy kates, reels, or niddy noddies.

The ultimate test of spinning a good yarn is in its fabrication and use. You may already be a weaver or a knitter, but chances are you are not both. And don't forget crocheting, tatting, bobbin lace, and other time-honored textile craft techniques. As you learn these methods of fabric construction, you will also be learning many more things about fiber properties, yarn properties, and fabric properties.

There is a nationwide, and even a worldwide, network of handspinners, who are eager to welcome you. Look for workshops, lectures, and conferences for handspinners in the calendar sections of the spinning-related magazines. Have fun. And spin a good yarn.

Spun from dyed flax by passersby at a commercial booth, this linen was brought together magnificently into a charming and machine-washable sweater.

A BREEZY LINEN SWEATER for Summer Spinning

Designed by Erika Baker

This sweater doesn't look like a sampler, but it is. The linen was spun by a variety of people who sat down at a demonstration wheel and "played" with the fiber. It was given to Erika Baker, who made this wonderful garment.

YARN: Handspun linen, two-ply at about 1375 yards per pound, in five shades.

GAUGE: 4 stitches = 1 inch, 8 rows = 1 inch, on size 4 needles.

NEEDLES: Straight needles in sizes 3 and 4, plus a 16-inch circular needle in size 3, or sizes required to produce correct gauge.

SIZE: Medium.

This sweater is made in two pieces, but an expert knitter could make it in one piece. The sweater is knitted sideways, starting at the arrows.

Front: *Begin at the front left side.* Using size 4 needles and the color you have chosen for your first stripe, cast on 80 stitches. Knit 26 rows in stockinette.

To change colors, you will knit a narrow stripe with a lace pattern (a total of 6 rows). Each narrow stripe will be knitted in the same color; in the sweater opposite, these stripes are white. Using white, knit 2 rows of stockinette. On the third row, * K2, K2 together, yarn over, and repeat from * across row. Knit 3 rows of stockinette.

Shape the neck. With your third color, knit 3 rows of stockinette. Decrease 1 stitch at the beginning of the following row. Repeat this decrease every other row 4 more times (75 stitches). Complete this stripe with 14 more rows (a total of 26 rows).

Knit another narrow stripe with the lace pattern. With your fourth color, knit a broad stripe (26 rows). Knit a third narrow lace stripe.

Complete the neck by changing to your fifth color and knitting 13 rows. Increase 1 at the beginning of the following row. Repeat this increase every other row 4 more times (80 stitches). Complete this stripe with 4 more rows (26 rows in all).

End with the front right side. Knit another narrow lace stripe, followed by a broad stripe (26 rows). Place 37 stitches from the top (the edge where the neck shaping occurred) on a holder, to be used for the armhole. On the remaining 43 stitches, work a narrow lace stripe. Bind off on the sixth row

Back: With the color used for the narrow stripes, cast on 43 stitches. Work the lace stripe. Change colors, knit across the 43 stitches, and cast on 37 more stitches. Work as for the front, eliminating neck shaping.

Finishing: Sew front to back at shoulder seams. Work the *neck edging* by picking up and knitting 96 stitches around the neckline; use the circular needle. Work 1 row of K1, P1 ribbing and then 1 row of the lace pattern (K2, K2 together, yarn over). Work 1 more row of ribbing and bind off loosely. For the *armhole,* use size 3 needles. On one side, you will have 37 stitches on a holder. Put these on a needle, and pick up and knit 37 stitches from the back. Work in K1, P1 rib, with 2 rows each of the colors you used (10 rows), binding off loosely on the last row. On the other side, pick up and knit 37 stitches on the front and 37 stitches on the back. Work as you did on the other side.

Join the sides by sewing together the remaining 43 stitches, starting at the waistline and finishing at the edge of the armhole. Work the *waistband:* using the color of the narrow stripes and the circular needle, pick up and knit 140 stitches around the waistline. Work K1, P1 twisted rib (on all knit stitches, insert tip of needle into *back* of stitch; throw yarn and complete stitch as usual) for 14 rows. Bind off on the 15th row. The twisted rib compensates somewhat for the non-stretchiness of linen fibers. You could also work special knitters' elastic into this ribbing.

This size yarn

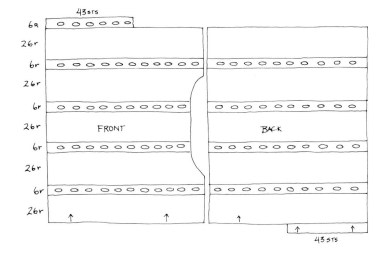

Appendix

Fleece Selection and Evaluation

When you have the opportunity to select your own raw fleece to process and spin, there are several things you can check to be sure the fleece is worth the asking price.

A new fleece may be presented to you still on the hoof, newly shorn but still open, rolled up neatly and tied with twine (tips in, shorn edges out), or stuffed in a big plastic bag. Some stores sell raw fleece in one-pound lots in plastic bags. You will be able to best evaluate the fleece if you can see it in one piece, unrolled, lying flat on the floor with the tips up. But you can still use many of the tests listed below if all you get to see is a small portion of the wool. A whole open fleece should look something like the photo opposite.

Take a look around the edges of the entire fleece. How much leg and belly wool is there, and how much dung are you paying for? A well-**skirted** fleece has had the shorter, coarser, dirtier leg and belly wool removed, as well as the **dung tags,** so that the weight of the fleece includes spinnable wool only. If it has not been well skirted, then negotiate for a lower price per pound.

Take a lock of wool from the neck or shoulder area to examine more closely. Here's how. Grasp the end of one lock tightly with your finger and thumb, while you hold down all the rest of the locks around it with your other hand. Pull the lock toward you quickly—it will separate from the fleece without disturbing the locks around it. The neck and shoulder wool is considered the best on the animal, so this lock should be the best that you'll see from the fleece.

How dirty is the tip? That's where most of the dirt will cling to the greasy wool. Some dirt at the tip is to be expected, but if it's caked on thickly and dried, it's going to be especially hard to remove. Fine fleeces will have that problem much more often than coarse fleeces, because fine fleeces have more grease. On medium and coarse fleeces, look to see if the tip is **weathered.** Is it so discolored and dry that you can easily pull bits off with your finger and thumbnail? That is not necessarily a reason to reject the fleece, but you might want to think twice about the rain of little bits of wool you'll get during processing, and the possibility of a slightly weaker yarn.

Inspect the rest of the length of the lock (the staple length) for dirt, seeds, burrs, hay, or remnants thereof. Ideally the lock will be clean except at its tip. Any barnyard trash you see there will have to be removed, and, unfortunately, scouring and carding remove only a small portion. The worst offenders are the seeds and burrs that embed themselves in the fibers. Big pieces of hay and grass are removed easily by hand, but the small and medium-sized pieces will stubbornly remain. Plan on a lot of time-consuming labor if you buy that fleece.

Near the bottom of the staple, at the shorn end, look for dark little bugs and their eggs attached to the fiber shaft. Those are sheep lice—pass that fleece up.

Look along the lock for a line of yellow stain, or especially a line of felting. In continuously wet condi-

The fleece on the top is clean. The slight discoloration will wash out. The bottom fleece is naturally a beautiful gray, but the seeds and straw may be difficult to remove. There are also two second cuts at the base of the lock.

tions, the sheep's skin will itch, and the process of scratching on rocks and fences will tangle and felt the fleece. Reject it out of hand—the felting process is not reversible. The yellow coloration may or may not come out. The severest stain can be caused by long-lasting damp conditions as well, and if the conditions persist, a rot can set in. The only way to know if the stain will come out or not is to wash the lock and see. Don't buy the fleece unless you can do that, or unless you can live with the mottled coloring you'll get, even if you dye the fiber.

It's not a bad idea to wash the lock anyway—I do that as a matter of practice now. You can see the true color and condition of the fleece much better that way.

Now take the lock between both hands, holding it firmly between your thumbs and the sides of your forefingers. Seesaw the staple back and forth to loosen the fibers from one another. If need be, separate the lock so that you are working with a piece no more than about half an inch in diameter. With steadily increasing pressure, pull both ends of the staple away from each other. Use firm pressure, but don't go overboard. If you have a sound and strong fleece,

nothing will happen. If the fleece has a **break** in it, you will feel fibers start to give way. Hold the lock up to your ear as you do the same thing, and you will be able to hear the fibers breaking. Hold the lock up to the light and you will probably see a thinning of fibers at the break. Pass this fleece by —it will break during processing and produce neps in your fiber preparation, and your yarn will be weak and full of short fibers. If the lock breaks all the way across in a straight line, then the animal had some sort of trauma, like a sickness or injury, at that point in the fleece's growth. If it breaks randomly, then the poor animal has had a tough time ever since last shearing.

In looking at the whole fleece, look on the shorn side for **second cuts.** This is where the shearer had to take a second pass with the shears because he did not come near enough to the skin the first time. Second cuts are to be avoided—they mean a shorter staple length for you to work with in that portion of the fleece, and little bits of wool that you'll have to remove by hand. If there are only a few, it won't be a big problem.

You may not always have the option of looking at the entire fleece; if you are buying at a fleece auction

If you acquire a whole fleece which has been shorn with the hand-spinner in mind, it will come in a rolled form with the cut ends of the locks facing out. If you gently unroll it, you will find that it was shorn in one piece and that it still retains the sheep's shape. You'll be able to find the leg wool, the neck section, and the tail portion. If the fleece has been skirted, as this one has, the dirtiest wool will have been removed from the edges of the fleece. This fleece is from a Karakul sheep. The wool is coarse and durable.

(such as at the county fairs) or through the mail, then the best you can hope for is seeing a representative lock. Find out as much as you can by examining that lock, and washing it if possible. If the fleece is rolled, check for second cuts, and try to take one or two more locks from other areas of the fleece. Be neat and respectful of the package, though, and leave the locks you take for the next spinner to examine—think of it from the seller's point of view.

Fleeces can weigh from just a few pounds to over fifteen pounds, depending on the breed. Know how much the fleece weighs so that you can multiply that figure by the price per pound.

Sorting

Some parts of the fleece will have a shorter staple length than others; some areas will probably have more crimp; some may feel coarser. You will want to separate the fleece into sections that contain wool of the same length, crimp, and softness, so that your yarn will be uniform. Use the different sections for different projects. The neck and shoulder wool is considered the best, the leg and belly wool the worst.

Scouring (Washing) Your Wool

Scouring seeks to remove wool grease, suint, dirt, vegetation, chemicals, and pests from your wool. Let's take a look at those one by one.

Wool grease (fat, wax) is chemically a wax, and
- is insoluble in water
- is deposited directly on the fibers as they grow
- has a melting point between 95° and 104° F (That's important to remember when you are drawing the scouring bath.)
- is found on both primary and secondary fibers. (Sheep have primary and secondary fiber follicles, related to the hairy outer coat and downy undercoat still found on the primitive breeds. After countless generations of selective breeding, the fibers produced from the two types of follicles on today's modern breeds are essentially identical. Many of the ancient breeds still retain this double-coated characteristic.)

Suint is composed mainly of potassium salts from dried perspiration, and
- is soluble in water
- is deposited on *top* of the wax as the fiber grows
- readily absorbs moisture from the air
- is found only on primary fibers
- can combine with wool grease in the presence of water to form a kind of soap.

Dirt includes
- sand, mud, and dust
- epidermal ''scurf'' (dry skin flakes)
- fragments of fiber root sheaths that break away as the fiber emerges.

Vegetation includes
- seeds
- burrs
- hay
- grasses
- fragments of the above.

Chemicals include
- pesticides
- medications
- dye markers.

The three things that you want to do in scouring your wool are (1) to get it completely clean, while you (2) avoid felting, and (3) avoid any alkaline damage.

1. Getting it Clean

The finer the fleece, the more grease it contains, and therefore the harder it is to get clean. When you have a hard-to-clean fleece, you are tempted to agitate and scrub more, which leads to felting, or to add harsher cleaning agents, which leads to alkaline damage. And the finer the fleece, the more susceptible it is to felting and to alkaline damage.

The solution is twofold: use *hot* water, so that the bath will not cool down too much as the wool sits and soaks, and use more detergent than you would for just about any other cleaning job. If you use the hot water right out of your tap, you'll find that it's probably somewhere between 120° and 140° F, hot enough to keep the temperature of the bath above the melting point of the grease while you work, but low enough to avoid damaging the fibers. And as for the use of more detergent, industry has determined that it takes *fifteen to sixteen times* the amount of detergent to remove wool grease than it does for other oils and greases. If you don't use a *lot* of mild detergent when you scour, you won't get out all the grease; the wool may feel clean initially, but a few weeks later the remaining grease will oxidize and become tacky. Trying to smoothly spin a fine, tacky wool is an exercise in frustration.

Wool wax, or lanolin, does not become rancid, unlike other organic fats, but it does dry out to a sticky consistency. Industry uses this property of lanolin to great advantage in the manufacture of adhesive tapes. Think about this when you are tempted to "leave some natural lanolin" in your washed fleeces for water repellency. The wool fiber's outer cuticle is already a naturally water-repellent surface. Leaving oils or grease on your wools is an invitation to rapid soiling.

And remember: even in industry's harsh scouring methods, about five percent of the grease is left in the wool. Hand scouring leaves even more. So feel free to be thorough in your washing, without any fear of drying out the fleece excessively.

2. Avoiding Felt

Felting requires moisture, heat, and agitation of the wool. A good scour requires moisture, heat, and agitation as well, in the presence of a detergent. But if you concentrate on getting the temperature of the water right, using enough detergent, and limiting agitation, you can get very clean, soft wool without felting. Step-by-step procedures are given on pages 109-111.

Some other things that you can do to avoid felting are to never run water directly on the wool, and never vary the temperature of the wash and rinse baths.

3. Alkaline Damage

Wool can be damaged in scouring liquors that exceed 9 or 9.5 on the acid/alkaline (pH) scale. Since most of us don't use pH testers, you can see that adding washing soda to the bath can be a dangerous proposition. Although it can add cleaning power, it is highly alkaline, and alkaline solutions above pH 9.5 "eat" wool.

Alkaline damage is irreversible. It is characterized by curling tips (especially at the shorn end), scale damage (even a dissolving of the scales) and a harsh hand.

Soaps and Detergents

Some scouring recipes recommend the use of pure soap to clean wool be-

cause of its mildness. But there are two problems with pure soaps. One is that you have to be darn sure that the soap flakes are *completely* dissolved before you enter the wool into the bath. If semi-dissolved flakes are still in the water, they stick to the wool, and for some reason subsequent scouring doesn't seem to remove them. Even worse, pure soaps will combine with calcium and magnesium in hard water, leaving insoluble precipitates, goopy little globs which tend to redeposit on the wool. They do not scour out. Once you've got them, you're stuck with them.

But all is not lost if you're in a hard-water area. All you have to do is use a mild liquid dishwashing detergent or its equivalent. They have something called "sequestrants" that bind up the minerals before the precipitates can form. Or you can use a water softener like Calgon, or any of the mechanical ion exchange systems.

Orvus WAS paste (sodium laurel sulfate) is a pure, mild, pH-neutral detergent. I like this very mild pure detergent for scouring. It is made of the same basic ingredient found in many shampoos. You can find it in gallon jugs at feed stores (4H kids use Orvus to clean their animals before a show). I don't recommend Woolite because its properties of suspension, lubrication, and protection of the fiber are less effective than some other detergents. Neither can I recommend laundry detergents—they have too many additives, some of them harsh.

Scouring Recipes

1. Carefully separate a piece of fleece of the same dimensions as your dishpan: Hold the tips of the locks firmly on either side of the place where you want the fleece to separate and pull them apart. Work neatly—don't let the fibers slide past one another and become disarrayed. Work your way around the section of fleece until it is free from the rest. Keep all the tips facing in one direction, and the shorn ends in the other.

2. Fill two dishpans with hot water right out of the tap. Add liquid dish-

washing detergent (or Orvus) to both pans until the water feels slick when tested with a clean dry hand. Do not make suds.

3. Turn the section of fleece on its side so that the tips will face the center of the dishpan and the shorn edges will face the side. Immerse the fleece slowly along the left edge of the first dishpan. Let it soak there for ten minutes.

4. With your left hand, push a section of wool down to the bottom of the pan. With your right hand, rub the tips of the locks of that same section of wool until they come clean. (You can agitate the tips of the locks as much as you want to, as long as the shorn ends don't move. Felting takes place at the shorn end.) Repeat until all the tips are clean.

5. With your right hand acting as a barrier so the wool doesn't try to slide around and move to the right, slowly gather up the wool toward you with your left hand until you can lift it gently from underneath, and let it drain there a bit as you hold it. Remember, wool is weaker when wet, so it must be well supported. You can squeeze the wool slowly and gently to help drain off the dirty, soapy water.

6. Put the wool in the second bath in the same position (that bath is the same temperature now as the first bath). Let the wool soak for another five or ten minutes, with no agitation at all.

7. Remove the wool as you did in step five, and set it aside. Drain and rinse the dishpans. Fill them with water the same temperature as the baths you just emptied, or slightly hotter. Add about three or four tablespoons of vinegar to the first bath (the amount is not critical; the vinegar will help cut the excess detergent and leave the wool in a slightly acid environment).

8. Put the wool in the first rinse bath in the same position, and gently push it down slowly until it is covered. Don't let the wool migrate all over the pan. Leave it there for five minutes, and then repeat in the second rinse bath.

9. Lift the wool carefully as in step five, gently squeeze out the excess water, and lay the wool on a clean dry towel to drain. Once the towel has soaked up a good deal of the water, you can speed drying by moving the wool to a fresh dry towel. Let it dry away from heat, sun, pets, and any further agitation on your part. Depending on the weather, it will dry completely in one to three days.

Scouring the wool this way will leave you with tips and shorn ends aligned, so that you can use the clean wool for carding or combing.

This washing sequence took you all the way through with one small section of the fleece, but you can set this up as a sort of wash train. If the fleece is not excessively dirty, you can use the first wash bath twice, and the successive baths as well, so that you have one wool section immediately following another. If the fleece is pretty greasy and dirty, you can just replace the first wash bath with the second, and make up a new second bath. Depending on how your facilities are set up, you can make adjustments to this procedure to save time, effort, and water.

If you have a very special fleece, either one that is very fine and delicate, or perhaps quite dirty at the tips, you may want to scour lock by lock. Use the same sequence as above but separate and handle the locks individually. Keep the shorn ends tucked tightly away in your hand while you scrub the tips. Let the just-scrubbed locks soak undisturbed in the second bath while you scrub the next lock in the first bath.

Oiling

Some spinners feel that oiling a clean fleece will make it easier to spin. I have never found that necessary—the fleeces that I use, carefully scoured in mild detergent, are soft and silky, and draft easily. But I can imagine working with an exceptionally dry fleece (perhaps from a breed that doesn't put out much wool grease and that has had a vigorous cleaning) that might be more pleasant to spin if oiled. If you do feel the need, fill a spritz bottle with half olive oil and half water. Spray the wool that you plan to spin in your next spinning session, put it loosely into a plastic bag in the sun, and let the water and oil penetrate to all parts of the fleece. Process and spin as usual. Don't let the oil get old on the fleece —use it while it is fresh. Be sure to wash and rinse your yarn.

Wheel Mechanics

You have already been introduced to the parts of the spinning wheel—the drive wheel, drive band, flyer, flyer shaft, flyer hooks, orifice, eye, bobbin, whorls, bearings, maidens, mother of all, axle, footman, and treadle. And you should have a pretty good idea now of how the flyer and bobbin rotate in relation to one another so that wind-on takes place. Something we didn't cover, though, was the part that *slippage* plays in the spinning and wind-on procedure.

On any wheel, no matter the type, either the bobbin or flyer must slip under the friction of the drive or brake band during certain phases of spinning. When you are holding the yarn under tension so that no wind-on takes place, the bobbin and flyer are rotating at the same speed—they are bound together by the tension on the yarn. Whichever element it is that normally slows during wind-on keeps up with the lead element by slipping. When you release tension on your yarn, slippage decreases dramatically, or stops altogether, and yarn is wound onto the bobbin.

Ratios

You may hear from other spinners, or see in spinning wheel ads, numbers that are referred to as the drive wheel ratio. They may be figures like 6 to 1, or 12 to 1, or 20 to 1. The ratio refers to how many turns the flyer makes (equalling how many twists are added to your yarn) for each revolution of the drive wheel. In the first example, each single rotation of the drive wheel makes the flyer rotate six times.

Using that same example, if you were to draft a one-inch length of yarn for every rotation of the drive wheel, your yarn would have six turns per inch (t.p.i.). If your yarn were very fine, that would probably not be enough to hold it together, but if your yarn were very thick, that much twist might make it kink and snarl. The size of your yarn, in combi-nation with the twists per inch, will determine its soundness and character.

You can see that to maintain a very even twist count in your yarn all you have to do is draft the same length each time you treadle. It might be one inch, three inches, or five inches, but as long as you do the same thing over and over, your yarn will be consistent, as least as far as twist goes.

When you are looking for a spinning wheel to purchase, the most versatile wheels will offer a range of drive ratios. A wheel with a range between about six and twelve is a good wheel for a novice spinner—you can start out with the lower slower ratios, and thicker yarns, and work up to the higher, faster ratios, and thinner yarns. Wheels that have ratios in the high teens and twenties, and even the thirties, are better suited to fast, experienced spinners.

If you don't know the ratio of a wheel, there is an easy way to measure it. Take a string and go around the drive wheel circumference. Where the string meets, make a mark on each end with a felt-tip pen. Measure the distance between the marks. Now do the same thing for the driven whorl (or the flyer whorl on a double drive wheel). Divide the whorl measurement into the drive wheel measurement, and that will give you the ratio. If there are several whorls, then do the calculation for each of them, and you'll know the range of drive ratios that you have available.

Oiling

You should oil the flyer shaft and the flyer bearings every time you change bobbins, or at least every hour of spinning. These parts need oiling most frequently because they turn at such rapid rates. The less you oil, the more friction there will be. That means rapidly wearing parts and more effort on your part to treadle. If you take a rag and wipe the bearings or shaft and the oil is black, then you haven't been oiling enough.

Every couple of hours of spinning you should oil the axle, both ends of the footman where it connects to the axle and the treadle (even if the connection is leather), and both pivots of the treadle.

Some wheels come with sealed bearings that do not require oiling. Oil the other surfaces that you can get to.

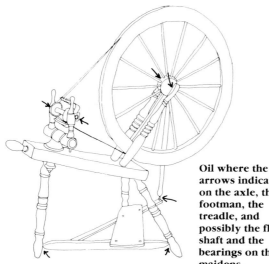

Oil where the arrows indicate: on the axle, the footman, the treadle, and possibly the flyer shaft and the bearings on the maidens.

When you first sit down at your wheel, if it has been several days since you last did any spinning, oil it everywhere as a matter of course.

Which oil? A lightweight oil such as sewing machine oil or 3-in-1 will do, but you will have to oil more often. I like to use 30-weight motor oil because of its heavier consistency. Some spinners use grease in the flyer bearings, but I find that 30-weight for all oiling works very well.

Buy a little oil can that has a long and very narrow spout so that you can oil down between the bobbin and flyer and other narrow spaces without taking everything apart. Keep a rag handy for wiping up excess oil. Just a drop or two will do—if you put too much oil on at once, it will spray out all over you and the room when you begin to spin.

Drive Cords and Brake Bands

Change your cotton drive cord when it gets dirty and sticky. The best material is a multi-ply cotton cord that

is soft and a bit fuzzy. Cut off your old cord to get the length measurement, then add a couple of inches extra to work with that you can cut off later. Set your wheel up so that the mother of all is set fairly close to the wheel—not all the way it will go, but enough in that direction so that any stretching of the new cord will still leave you plenty of adjusting room.

If your drive wheel is not removable, put the cord around the drive wheel and the driven element(s). Check its placement, cinch it up, and mark where you want the knot or splice to come together. Then move the maiden in toward the wheel to give yourself a little slack to work with. The best thing to do is either to splice or to sew the drive cord together firmly. If you just tie a knot, you will notice a vibrating bump every time the drive band goes around the bobbin or flyer whorls —it's annoying and can affect the smooth spinning of your yarn. If your drive wheel is removable, you can measure the new cord, splice or sew it while it's off the wheel, and then install it.

Cut a cord longer than you need. Put it in position and overlap the ends. Draw a line to mark the length you need.

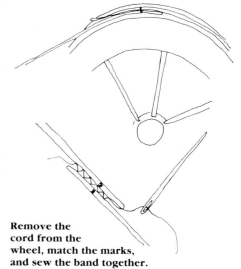

Remove the cord from the wheel, match the marks, and sew the band together.

If for some reason you need a new plastic drive band for wheels that come with those, see your dealer or the wheel manufacturer.

Brake bands are made of leather or some sort of string. The string bands are the ones you will need to replace occasionally. Waxed linen or waxed nylon serves the purpose very well. The cord will become frayed from friction with the whorl after a time, so when you put on new brake band material (just follow the path of the original band), put on more than you will initially need, so it can be moved and adjusted as it becomes worn.

If there is a stiff spring or a rubberband used for tension on the brake band, replace it with a lightweight spring from the hardware store. The more supple the spring, the more precise your control over the brake band tension will be.

Storage and Care

Check the orifice every once in a while for a buildup of fibers and dust. Clean it out with a cotton swab. Keep the surface of the flyer shaft free from fibers and dirty oil. Wipe the axle clean every now and then if you can get to it and apply fresh oil.

Keep your wheel out of direct sun, away from the damp, in moderate unchanging temperatures. Cover it if it needs to be stored for any time. If your wheel has been painted, varnished, or lacquered, then just wiping it down with a clean cloth occasionally will keep it looking good. If the surface was stained and/or oiled, then you should occasionally apply an additional coating of wax or furniture oil to keep the wood from drying out too much.

Shopping for a Wheel

Some of the things you should consider when thinking about purchasing a wheel include what kind of yarn you would like to spin; reliability, repairability, and versatility of the wheel; cost; the reputation of its maker; available accessories (a lazy kate, more bobbins, more flyer whorls); where you will be when you spin; realistic expectations about what wheels can do; and aesthetic preferences in look and design.

Most beginners don't yet know what kind of yarn they want to spin—that's fine, just look for a versatile wheel that you can spin on now and grow into. If you want to spin heavy yarns for outerwear or even rugs, then get a wheel with a large orifice and flyer, and big bobbins. The drive wheel itself needn't be big, because you will not need many twists per inch. If you prefer gossamer yarns, then you need a small orifice (small yarns vibrate in a big orifice as you spin), small flyer and bobbins, and many hooks on the flyer. The drive wheel shouldn't be too small, or you will be treadling like mad to get enough twist in each length of yarn. Don't forget to think about the plied yarns you will want to make—can the wheel accommodate the size of those as well?

As for reliability and repairs, find out who the manufacturer or builder is, where they live, and what kind of reputation they have. Most wheel makers are happy to make any repairs necessary, but others are hard to track down and reluctant to attend to ''old business''. Check on the wheel maker's schedule as well—when can he deliver? For hand-crafted wheels you may have to wait months; for factory-made wheels, you'll probably be able to buy them directly off the floor at a spinning shop.

If you are going to be traveling to guild meetings, spinning workshops, or historical exhibitions, then you want a very small, compact wheel to take with you. You won't be able to spin as much yarn in the same amount of time as on a bigger wheel, but at least you can take it with you. If you are going to do all your spinning in your home with the wheel in one spot, then portability is not a concern.

If you buy a used wheel, best buy it from another spinner, and sit down and try it out yourself. If it's an antique, it may not have all the parts required, it may be difficult to get spare parts, and you may not be able to tell if it will work when it's repaired.

When you begin to look at ads in the magazines and at the wheels in spinning and weaving shops, you'll notice that there is quite a diversity in design. Some look thoroughly modern, and some are reproductions of antique designs. Some are sleek and elegant, some are very ornate. Some are just cute. It *is* important to like what you see, because you are going to be sitting in front of this wheel for some time to come, and pass it by innumerable times on your way through the living room. But it's much more important how the wheel *works*—neither modern concepts in design nor antique-like turnings guarantee that a wheel will perform well. Decide first if you can spin comfortably and efficiently on the wheel, and only then choose it for its good looks.

I have never come across a wheel that can do it all. The very best advice I can give you is to try out the wheel for yourself. One ten-minute trial isn't really enough. Spin on the wheel for thirty or forty minutes at least, and spin as many different kinds of yarn on it that you can, including plies. Make every kind of adjustment, and use every size of whorl that you can. If you don't feel experienced enough to do it yourself, then take an experienced spinner with you. (Even an experienced spinner needs a few minutes just to get used to a new wheel—every wheel has its own touch and idiosyncracies.) Ask advice from spinners in your local guild. Look at what kind of yarn they spin and how they spin it. Ask if you can try out their wheels for a while. And look at the ads with a wee bit of skepticism—if you see a wheel that's advertised as being the wheel that can do everything, or the wheel that eliminates the need for fiber preparation or spinning skill, don't believe it.

Sitting Down to Spin

When you are ready to try out the wheel, here are a few things to look for. Sight down the rim of the wheel as you give it a spin. The wheel should ride straight and true, and not wobble or throw off the drive band. What does the groove in the drive wheel look like? If it's polished and smooth, the drive band won't get as good a grip, and you'll have to work with greater drive-band tension. Same thing goes for the bobbin and flyer whorls.

Make sure the wheel has been oiled recently or oil it yourself. Sit down and get yourself comfortable, adjust the drive-band tension, and then begin to treadle without spinning. Watch the flyer and bobbin. Do they vibrate? Make clicking noises? At what speed? The bobbin and flyer assembly should rotate rapidly and smoothly even at high speeds—this is an indication that they have been balanced.

Are there hooks on both sides of the flyer? You want them there to balance the flyer. How hard is it to remove the flyer and bobbin? Give it a try and see. Work all the adjustment mechanisms—tensioning and braking devices. If the wheel is removable, remove it yourself to see what's involved. See how far the wheel breaks down, if at all, for shipping or traveling.

How well is the wheel made? Are there rough edges or a careless application of finish? Are you pleased by the care and attention that has been put into making this a fine tool?

Now take out some wool and start spinning. Try thick, thin, and medium yarns, as you vary the drive- and brake-band tensions. Bring along some singles of different sizes to ply on the wheel. Does your yarn jump and vibrate at the orifice? The orifice may be too large for the yarn you are spinning, or the flyer and bobbin assembly may not be balanced. Is the wheel hard to treadle even after oiling? New drive and brake bands might help. Does the toe of the treadle sink lower than the heel at its lowest point of travel? That might put too much strain on your ankle after a short time. Is the wheel yanking the yarn out of your hand no matter how loose you adjust the take-up tension? Then you won't be able to spin fine yarns on this wheel, though it may be very efficient for medium and thick yarns.

Now taking everything you have learned into consideration, what is the cost? Can you grow into this wheel, or does it barely suit your purposes now? Are additional parts easy to come by?

Go and try as many other wheels as you can. The more you try, the more you'll learn, and the happier you'll be with your final purchase.

Sources

Spin·Off, a quarterly magazine for handspinners. *Spin·Off* also offers a continually updated list of spinning guilds across the U.S. and in other countries. Interweave Press, 201 East Fourth Street, Loveland, Colorado 80537. (303) 660-7672. Also publishers of *Handwoven* and numerous books related to the textile field.

Black Sheep Newsletter, 30781 Fox Hollow Road, Eugene, Oregon 97405.

Shuttle Spindle & Dyepot, quarterly magazine of the Handweavers Guild of America. Membership in the HGA includes subscription. Shuttle Spindle & Dyepot, 2402 University Avenue, Suite 702, St. Paul, Minnesota 55114. (612) 646-0802.

The publications listed above carry ads for suppliers of tools, fibers, and dyes. The dyed batts and pencil roving and the carded rovings onpages 57 and 68 were supplied by Alden Amos, of Jackson, California. the fleece on page 66 was imported from New Zealand and hand-dyed by Otter Lodge, of Fort collins, Colorado. The dyed linen used to make the sweater on page 104 came from Euroflax, of Rye, New York. the fleece on page 107 was provided by Bliss Natural Colored Sheep and Fleeces, of Loveland, Colorado.

Index